JUST **BRAND YOU**™

Unlock your full potential and transform your business by building a brand that looks, feels and sounds like you.

NICKI LOUISE JAMES

CONTENTS

For Betty.
Who taught me to pay my strengths forward. Who
helped me to realise that all of this was possible. Who
made me who I am today. I am not the only one
helping the ladies reading this book. You can take
credit for some of that.

Always part of the journey.

Your legacy lives on.

INTRO

Hey, you absolute beauty...

First off, I want to say how excited I am that you've picked this book up off the shelves, been gifted this or even better, it's been recommended to you. I love the idea of this book being the type of book you pass around to your business besties or maybe you are just going to keep it to yourself because it's going to be your brand bible from now on. It's been a long time coming, that I've wanted to put pen to paper and finally it's arrived.

I didn't want to create a boring, stereotypical brand book. That's just not my style. I wanted something different, but I feared that I wouldn't be able to find a unique way of positioning my book to others in the same genre. Which is quite funny really as my entire business is all about being unique, standing out and building a brand with you at its heart. It's about finding your own way of saying things and your own way of doing things so that you stand out in the sea of sameness. Yet, when I came to write this, the fear of saying the same old stuff just came to the surface, because we all have wobbles, especially when it comes to brand related things and pushing ourselves out of our comfort zones. I bet you do too. And the truth is... that ain't ever gonna change. So, yes, I could talk to you about just logos and websites and all the fancy bits. Or overwhelm you with letter spacing, line height and a load of code jargon that neither of us are going to understand: you know, the stereotypical parts of a brand identity or the top ten ways to nail that killer website. But even though they are huge parts of it and I will guide you with some of these things, there is so much more to building a successful brand.

So how do we do that? Well, first off we need to stop thinking of our branding as our brand. They are two very different things. To be precise, your branding is your visuals and a brand is every single thing you put out there from now on. It's the essence, the character and the truth behind who you are as a woman. And I need to get this crystal clear right at the start because more and more I see entrepreneurs who think they've nailed it, just because they've got the visuals in place. But the visuals aren't the most important bit, because if the foundations aren't right or the brand doesn't evolve with you then it becomes stagnant. And the only way to build a standout brand is for you to be at its centre. But don't worry: I'm gonna walk you through it all.

My favourite part of what I do? Seeing the penny drop when my clients nail all of the elements; the clarity it can cause; and I wanted to be able to package that up and deliver it to you with a little bow. It's taken me years to get this far, but I've finally developed my signature Just Brand You™ system, which I am going to walk you through in this book, so that you can take it step by step and truly build that stand out brand. It works on these three things.

DEFINE BRAND YOU - Identifying who you are as a woman and in turn a brand and showing you how to define it and express it, but most importantly communicate it with the world.

BECOME BRAND YOU - The language you use, tone of voice you have and how you visually represent yourself. How we create all of the elements to ensure you have a brand that looks, feels and sounds like you.

LIVE BRAND YOU – Well, I guess this one is a bit obvious. It's how you continue to live it day in and day out. Because brands live forever. They grow with you. And you need to show up with intent every, single, day.

JUST BRAND YOU™

DEFINE BRAND YOU

Identifying who you are as a woman and in turn a brand and showing
you how to define it and express it, but most importantly communicate
it with the world.

BECOME BRAND YOU

The language you use, tone of voice you have and how you visually
represent yourself. How we create all of the elements to ensure you have
a brand that looks, feels and sounds like you.

LIVE BRAND YOU

Well, I guess this one is a bit obvious. It's how you continue to live it day
in and day out. Because brands live forever. They grow with you. And
you need to show up with intent every, single, day.

So this isn't a "read it" and "leave it" type of book. For you to get the most from it you need to not only read it, you need to digest it, scribble in it, highlight it, but also take the action and do it. You can do it in steps, put it down, pick it up again, use it as you will. I've sectioned off brand journal notes in the teachings so that you can go away and do the things.

And how do I know it works? Well, it's the exact steps I've taken in order to get myself into the position I am in right now. It's what made me an expert in my field and it's all the steps I take to help my clients do the same. It's been tried and tested, it's got the results and I want it to do the same for you.

You see, I get it. I've been there and I know what it's like to be on the cusp of an amazing business, but something isn't quite right and you spend all of your time looking at everyone else and wondering why they seem to have it all together and you are left floundering around and fighting for your clients' attention. Well, I am here to tell you, lovely, that you are your brand and the second you take these steps and start believing in yourself, it will all change for you.

But remember, your brand never stops. It's continuous and there is no A to B, quick fix solution. So live it, breathe it, adapt with it, grow with it and you can keep coming back to the bits you need, when you need them. There's no such thing as perfect. We've just got to start.

It's time to become the face of your business... let's do this.

DEFINE

BRAND

YOU

01

LITTLE GIRLS SHOULD BE SEEN AND NOT HEARD

I.AM.ME. Well, Nicki. And I thought I should start by introducing myself... That way you can see what is possible, how you too can pay your strengths forward and how you can build a business that helps and serves people all while being yourself. But also how this little girl who on paper shouldn't be where she is today has overcome obstacles and grown as an expert in her field, teaching and championing others to do the same. Let me show you how, if you pay your strengths forward, start celebrating what makes you different and show up to the world, only the best things can happen. It's unbelievable how many people out there need you. It's just that you haven't got in front of them and told them yet. It's time to create brand success and it all starts with you... or in this case, me.

I want to take you back to an age old saying that I've heard time and time again: "Children should be seen and not heard." Please tell me you've heard this. It can't just be me. I bet you've even been told it. And it's so funny, because I didn't even think it was a thing anymore. Obviously I am walking around with rose tinted glasses on. But I really struggle to understand that we still believe that children, with all their potential, our future, are being told to be quiet and to not have a voice or opinion, being told from a young age their voice doesn't matter. Imagine what effect this is having on them, on us, the ones who have heard it so many times and how we must all be bringing those age old sayings through into the adult aspects of our lives. How what we are told as children or as young adults lives with us, probably for the rest of our lives. The thought patterns we must be creating that are stopping us from being our true selves, from saying what we want to say and doing what we truly want to do.

And the funny thing is, I remember having this exact conversation when I spoke to my Mum about a talk I was writing in early 2020, all about how "Little girls should be seen and not heard" and straight away she turned around completely straight faced and said to me, "Damn right, too." Then the little smirk came out as she knew instantly she'd pushed my buttons. And she knows what happens when I get a little bit ranty pants. On this occasion, I let it slide. Because I honestly don't think she meant it in a nasty way, and she didn't mean it to cause any offence, but it's been ingrained into her by her parents and for them by theirs and you can imagine how this list goes on. I mean, it dates right back to Victorian times, when children were hit with rulers for speaking out of turn, for not conforming to what a child "should be". So I guess I can't blame my Mum for having this reaction. All she was doing was paying what she had been told many times herself forward to me. Just as many parents for generation after generation have done the same.

But what really IS out of turn? And can we honestly still be peddling this sh*t? Are we honestly living in a society where children are told to be quiet because it is an inconvenience to us if they are not? Well, for me that's probably where best to start my story...

I was brought up in the 90s, a time of the Spice Girls (I always wanted to be Ginger Spice - obvs!) and Furbies - do you remember those? I would spend many a Christmas with a new Spice Girls sweater on. You know, the cheesy ones with all five of them on the front. Sporty doing a high kick, Ginger Spice basically showing her crotch and Baby Spice twiddling her pigtails in a cutesy kind of way. But I loved it, I was obsessed! A proper fan girl. And it went as far as me parading around with my eldest brother - fifteen years my senior to be precise, poor bloke, dancing to their latest album which I believe at the time was Spiceworld - legendary album. So here's me, hairbrush in hand, my best fancy dress princess shoes on (you know the ones, big bows, sparkles, glitter) and dictating to my brother, hands on hips, that once again he got the *Stop Right*

Now moves wrong. I had all the sass, showing him for the umpteenth time how you point over the right shoulder before your left. How did he not get it?

So I guess you could say, I had gumption. I was born to be in front of people and I was always a happy little kid. Inquisitive, playful and really loving. I'd be the type of kid who opened up her bag of sweets and shared them round the room and I would ALWAYS give away my last Rolo. Only to the selected, 'bestest' people, of course. I've just always wanted to be loved and have always loved those closest to me fiercely.

But the phrase 'children should be seen and not heard' was used in a very different way for me. So different once I found my voice, once I learnt to ask *"why"* all the time and when I insisted on running up and down the stairs again and again because I hadn't brought another one of my favourite Barbies down to the make-believe tea party around the dining table. See, this phrase sums up probably some of the most difficult times of my life. But the thing is, at the time, as much as I may have cried or felt really sorry for myself for a short while, I didn't really realise that what was happening behind the closed doors of my childhood was different to that of a normal little girl. I didn't realise it was so, so wrong. Because to me, what was happening was just normal, so how could it not be what I deserved? How was it now a way I should be punished for my "bad behaviour?" And deep down I think I felt that I was being the inconvenience; I was causing the problem; I should have been better. Been less Nicki. So I kind of deserved it. And actually, if I'd have just behaved, sat down, kept myself to myself and was a little less loud and a little less playful and maybe even a little less loving, then perhaps some of the things that happened in my childhood would never have happened to me.

You see, my Dad was a tormented alcoholic, a Jekyll and Hyde type character, who loved you one minute and the next you'd be seeing a very different person. I can't say that all of my memories of him are negative ones, as that would be unfair. I do remember many happy memories of his Elvis impressions (God, they were awful) and dancing around on his shoulders to the Eastenders cast singing old folk songs round a piano. Or perhaps my favourite thing of getting him to change my dolls' clothes and restyling their hair (my brothers got roped into that too). But there was always something that went wrong. Those experiences never lasted for too long. It would always feel like a bit of a dream before the reality truly kicked in.

A debt collector would show up and Mum and I would hide under the front door, or he'd lose his temper, or worse. And it all hit a bit of a crescendo when my Mum was at work over the holidays and he became my full time carer. See it was then that he had to be a proper Dad, a full-time parent, while Mum brought home the bacon. I guess he just couldn't cope with having a six year old little girl running around. And part of me can sympathise with him now. I mean you remember going out on a night out, having too much booze and waking up the next day like a bear with a sore head and even your partner next to you saying "Morning" makes you feel like you've been hit round the head with a frying pan. Well, I guess for Dad that was a regular feeling and his coping mechanism was to pick up the bottle and drink a little bit more.

I was always punished for making too much noise and I guess to him I probably sounded like a pneumatic drill. But it's only when I look back now that I actually realise a lot of this wasn't my fault. I was just being that dopey little performer that a lot of little girls are. I was inquisitive and excitable and all the things most people love about their children, or at least tolerate, even if it does sometimes get on your nerves. And it was all of these things my Mum actually loved about me and encouraged in me. But they weren't okay for my Pa. They were an inconvenience when he'd had a belly full of whatever booze he could get his hands on that morning and he dived into that big black hole. It was in those times that I was expected to sit there, be quiet and see to myself, either that or accept the consequences of my actions.

I can still picture now one occasion when Mum wasn't home and Dad needed to go out to get his latest stash or see a fancy woman or two and I was under strict instructions to have lunch made when he got home. Dad was a good cook, so I was honoured I'd been entrusted with such an important task. Ham and cheese sarnies with white crusty bread. My favourite. I'd never really cooked on my own. I'd never really had to, but I was up for the task. Obviously now I know at the age of six being asked to make lunch and being left home alone wasn't actually ok. But back then, I saw it as a privilege. Unfortunately, lunch didn't quite go to plan. Even today I can't butter bread (an ongoing joke in our household - don't even ask) and Mum never let me use sharp knives so the bread looked more like an old lady's doily than it did a nice appetising slice and the cheese, oh my, the cheese, it might as well have been the entire block straight out of the packet. The ham went ok though, that was already sliced, so I managed that bit okay.

I can picture what happened next right now, as if it was yesterday. We always entered the back of the house when we came home and here came Dad, blue bag from the offie in one hand and a walk that could only resemble someone who was struggling on choppy seas. That moment just before you puke and you are feeling rough as anything. I didn't realise and beamed from ear to ear, knowing it wasn't perfect but pleased with my efforts. like a giddy little girl, ready to show off my best work. Unfortunately, we had very different thoughts on the matter. In that moment I saw his entire facial expression change. Like when you see a traffic light go from green to an amber warning sign and if you were to drive through it then you better get ready because there is danger ahead. He lost it, quite rightly so I guess, because the kitchen was a tip, we were losing money like wildfire from all his dodgy dealings and *I'd just wasted half the sandwich ingredients!*

He came towards me, one step, two step. It felt like slow motion. He picked up the knife from the knife block, shouting, swearing, swerving and that was it, he had me. Knife in hand, he pushed me, back against the wall. "You fucking idiot, look what you've done! Do you not think my life is hard enough?"

I was so sorry. I felt the tears running down my cheeks and I was motionless. I couldn't move.

"Do you hear me?" he screamed. And in that moment of pure rage, a light came on and he realised what he was doing. What he had done. I watched a broken man collapse to the floor and my guilt became enormous. If only I'd done it right, if only I'd been better. If only I could have said something in that moment, taken the blame. So that he wouldn't be in front of me as he was right now, a man that I loved so much. It wasn't the first time; goodness, it wasn't the last, but as I said, times weren't all bad and at the time, although I was scared I don't know if as a child I thought this was normal for being what felt like a complete imbecile.

Given this kind of start in life, things could have turned out very differently for me. As it stands, I've got a really successful business, I'm happily married to the most amazing man in the world, the only person I've ever let in to look after me, and life is pretty stable. But it hasn't always been that way. It's not always been this easy. I found it so difficult to make friends and build relationships in my younger years. I found myself having them and losing them quite quickly. I can remember many a time feeling a little bit awkward, almost envious, when it came to visiting friends' houses and seeing their amazing relationships with their fathers who seemed to absolutely idolise them and I always wondered why I didn't have the same. But we'd left my Dad by this point and it was just me and my Mum and we did okay. We were each other's rocks and we got by. It wasn't always easy, but life was a damn sight calmer.

I think when you go through adversity at a young age, it always has an impact on you. I still can't really put my finger on the reason why, but I started getting bullied for being different. I was called a teacher's pet because I got my head down and cracked on. It was easier that way for me. And I actually generally liked learning. I'm a firm believer that the day I stop learning in life is the day I need to change paths, do something different, challenge myself again.

I got picked on because of my hairy arms. I even shaved it off one time and looked utterly ridiculous as they grew back as stubble. My Mum shook her head saying, "They'll grow back thicker, you know." And of course, that gave the kids in the playground something else to laugh at. But the worst one that still sticks with me today as I look at my brand photos or watch my lil' mug on a Facebook Live was being called 'shrew'. I've got a bit of a ski-slope nose with a little bobble on the end. Mum used to describe it as my cherry on the top, but kids just loved that at school! Unfortunately, I couldn't cut my nose off and I wasn't about to go under the knife, so that one's stuck.

But despite all this, I think as a child I was lucky. I know that not everyone, like me, has someone to show them that paying your adversity forward isn't the only way.

OR THAT YOU DON'T HAVE TO BE A PRODUCT OF YOUR PAST. YOU GET TO DICTATE THE PATH YOU TAKE IN YOUR FUTURE.

Let me introduce you to my biggest cheerleader, my Grandma, Betty. A jolly lady, that almost looked a bit owl like; quite coincidental really, given her wisdom. Betty was never shy of giving her opinions. Betty was totally okay with being seen and heard. And she'd let you know that was the case. You see, my Grandma was the kind of woman who'd tell you how it was and then some. You can imagine, can't you? And as she got older, she'd be forever complaining that people weren't doing things the *"done way"* (also known as: her way). She'd moan and moan about people leaving their washing in the machine of her warden controlled communal washing area, which was just utterly unacceptable. "What about others?" she'd say.

And I can picture to this day her nuisance neighbour a few flats up, who always hung around in a strange manner outside her door and cast shadows in the window pane so she knew she was there. It came to a point where she would start shouting at the door for her to "piss off," despite my absolute horror when I stayed for a trip at Granny's on the fold out mattress on the floor. But she didn't care, because she wasn't going to be imposed on. She was always gonna say it how it was.

But the best thing about Gran was that for all her funny little strong-minded quirks, she'd ALWAYS be the person that, when sh*t hit the fan, would be there with open arms giving you a big Granny cuddle and telling you it was all going to be ok. She became the main person I spoke to about how I was feeling. Not because I couldn't speak to my Mum because I could. But Mum was dealing with a lot herself and Gran, well, she was a listener. A solution maker. And a good teller off-er if you needed to hear it. I sit here now writing this chapter and see her wagging her crooked little arthritic finger as she told you her opinion on how doing it her way would be the best solution. Or that you are just "totally wrong and should respect your elders." But something I must tell you about Betty is that she too was silenced in her youth by violence and abuse, but like me, she wasn't going to let it stop her being the strong confident woman that she ended up being. She paid her strengths forward and taught me to do the same.

What she made me realise when I look back now, is that *this* is completely the strength we have as women, as a community, as business people. We have the power to make a change in people's lives. We get to choose how we show up for our audience, how we decide to be ourselves and how we help others in doing so. We get to decide who we are, who we want to be and no one can tell us otherwise. We can utilise our stories and what we've been through to help others. We can inspire change and to use it as a driving force for everything we do.

I wouldn't be standing here today if it wasn't for her.

I remember one of the last things she said to me before she passed. "You are more than this 9-5, Nicola," and at the time I had zero clue what she was talking about. I loved my job. I'd worked for so many amazing brands and magazines. I'd finally found a job I was super happy in after bouncing back from many redundancies, so why did she think I had more to give? It made no sense at the time but I guess if I look back now, she could always see what others do now: that I am a helper. All I want from my business is to be able to empower women to be true to themselves, to realise that they have all the power sitting there inside them. I want to have an impact. So for that... I'm gonna raise a glass to my Gran, Betty. Raise your mugs, ladies!

Those words stuck in my head. Maybe I do have more to give? Maybe this 9-5 isn't all I am cut out for. I knew I had drive and I knew I had ambition and I always wanted more, to be more. And finally I think I've found my place to shine. Over the years, I've helped so many female entrepreneurs dig a bit deeper, to show a bit more of them and to pull down that barrier or facade of who they think they need to be as business women. We can try to be like everyone else: we can look at what everyone else is doing, or we can look inside ourselves. Because every woman has a hidden superpower, a secret ingredient that makes them different from anyone else that does what they do. Every single person I work with has inner strengths, no matter what their business - service or product based. The problem is there is always another reason for the fact that they are not showing it, whether it's from their past, from something they've experienced or been told or it could be something that is going on right now. But we have to choose to not let that hold us back. We have to choose to help people. We have to choose to be seen, choose to be heard and choose to be us.

And you know what? You have that power too, otherwise you wouldn't be reading this book. We should no longer be living in a society where our strengths as individuals can't be paid forward. Where we hide them away in fear of being judged. Where children, women, minorities, entrepreneurs are told to not have an opinion, to be quiet and to be seen and not heard. Where we fear saying what we truly want to say because we think someone might not like it. Or worse, we might be judged. Told we are wrong. You see, it might have started when we were younger with a little old saying, but we've taken it into society and it shows on a daily basis.

Your story might not be the same as mine. It might not even have this tragic twist. But we've all got something. Something that's stopping us wanting to go for this full throttle. And it's time that changed. It's time to embrace your inner superwoman. It's time to show her to the world.

02

A LITTLE MORE YOU AND A LOT LESS THEM.

Let me introduce you to Betty Lou Design, my first business that I started back in January 2016, inspired as you can imagine by my Grandma, Betty. I can't even tell you the number of times that I was asked, "Are you Betty?" and I'd just smile and remember the reason why I started this. Quickly followed by a "Uhm... do I look like a Betty? I'm a 26 year old woman for Pete's sake." I don't know why but Betty always strikes me as a name for a jolly lady, carrying her knitting needles, who has one of those super infectious belly laughs that lights up the room. I might just be describing my Grandma there. But people asking me if this was my name wasn't all bad, as it did call for good conversation. It would follow on to them asking me why on earth I picked that name for my business if it wasn't my name and I had a great story to tell. I could tell them all about my Gran and those lovely memories and how she inspired me and they would *ooh* and *aaah* and it painted a picture. This in turn got them thinking of their loved ones. And the best bit was that it created a connection

15

in an instant. A relatability. An in. As all good stories do.

So as I said in Chapter One, my Gran knew I had more in me than my 9-5 and she was right. Within seven months and a lot of long, long nights handwriting envelopes, creating bespoke artwork and wax sealing envelopes for my clients, I left my 9-5 as an Art Editor. I remember chatting to Rob, my husband, about when my goal was to leave. I am one of those people who, if you give me a goal and a place I am going to get to, I will do it, no matter what it takes. I always thought it would be a year *at least* until that was even a possibility, but I just couldn't do it anymore. It was exhausting and I loved the idea of entrepreneurial life. And why not? I was making more money than I'd ever made in my 9-5, three times the amount to be exact and I just knew that it was time to take the leap. God, it was scary, but my oh my, it was worth it. I set up my home office on the dining room table (as we all do when we first start out) and I became a full time business woman. Was it easy? No. Was it rewarding...? Hell, yes!

I still remember now, members of my family saying I was from a different world now I was making more money. As if I'd changed in some way. Become someone different. I remember the feeling in the pit of my stomach when it was first said with others remarking that they'd all been speaking about it. Why did they all think that with success came change? Why did I suddenly feel like I didn't fit in with my own family? Because I don't think with any level of success or growth came rapid change in who I was as a person. I still love the same things. I might like staying in swanky hotels now because I can afford them, but you'll also find me gobbling a cheeky KFC drive thru on a trip home from a family do. Because you know what, I don't think money has to change us. I may earn more now and seem to have a knack of being successful, of building relationships with people and in return it's grown my business to, if I'm honest, a place I never thought was possible.

So I guess all this growth and quick success makes my business sound all sunshine and roses, right? Like there was a magic wand that got waved over me and bam! I just became successful. Like it was handed to me on a plate and I just sat back and enjoyed the ride. Well, it wasn't. I've been there, done the hustle, dealt with the tricky clients and let me tell you, it was really hard work. It's not just about doing the creative stuff. The things you love. Running a business is hard. The continuous social media, the accounts, the tax, the t&cs... *the boundaries!* You know where I am going with this. All the stuff we hate dealing with. And it's in those times that you need a support network around you because it gets lonely out there.

You start to reach out and try and make connections with other like-minded entrepreneurs, but making that kind of money so quickly in the wedding industry drew attention. And not necessarily always the kind you wanted. I remember several stationers saying to me, "It's not possible to make the money you make doing what we do," or, "How do you do it?" and, "But there is an industry standard and people don't pay over a certain amount for wedding stationery." As if there was some form of rule book to follow for anyone in the industry whereby it states that you can only charge a certain amount and if you break the rules then you are out. Exiled. Judged, for maybe having found a little gap in the market and working it. The problem is, that being in the wedding industry made me feel that to fit in I forever needed to put myself back in my box and it caused some real anxiety around what I could and couldn't do. I felt forever judged for doing things a bit different, my way. So even though I was doing it really well, the overarching feeling was that it sucked!

It kind of felt like being at school: you know, when you have the popular girls at the top? Well, in the stationery world there seemed to be an elite group of women who'd been in it for longer and had the most success, so if someone else came around and made a bit of noise it created a stir.

Over time, it meant I fell out of love with something that I was so passionate about. That and the arthritic fingers that I could see coming a mile off from addressing yet *another* handwritten envelope. So was it all really worth it? It started to make me question why I'd even started because if I had to fit in to some norm then I just wasn't sure I'd ever fit in. If I couldn't do it differently and I didn't like how it was being done, then why do it at all? And I remember that complete and utter breakthrough moment. I decided to niche down and stand the hell out. I decided I wouldn't be told how I could act and what I could do. I wanted to work in a certain way, with certain people, and I found a new crowd of cheerleaders on the internet. And it grew.

Suddenly, I was the go-to stationer for a select group of planners. I was recommended for my skills, but it still felt very much like I was always beneath people. Or so I told myself. But most importantly, I still wasn't making enough difference in the world. It still wasn't enough. I still had more in me. I was just dying to give more. I'd got the entrepreneurial bug. And I loved it. But in the stationery world I'd hit a ceiling of what I could achieve.

I am a firm believer in investing in yourself if you want to get ahead, if you want to be more. You can't always do that alone. You need more eyes on the business, a bird's eye view of where the gaps are. I remember meeting my business coach Lisa for the first time. I was trying to pitch her wedding stationery over a glass of prosecco at The Hospital Club and it turned out we both had other ideas.

It was like being star struck. I'd been following this woman online for months and she actually said yes to meeting me. Me! But it was this one meeting that changed my life forever. Instead of a new wedding stationery order, I walked out with that nervous, butterfly feeling in my chest, and straight away called my husband... we needed to find £4k. He said, "Well, it doesn't really matter what I say, does it? You are going to do it anyway and if you feel it's going to pay off then go for it." That one line is now a running joke in our household as he always wonders why I ask him, but I just think it's polite to run it past him and then do what I want anyway.

It was then, during this coaching, that I realised how much more I had to give. How I could serve in a much bigger way. It was like she had this hidden magic that saw the potential in people. We looked at my skills and my strengths and finally I got to pay my real strengths forward. I really got to make a difference and I really got to change people's lives. I could help women with all I'd learnt along the way to stand out, be bold, attract more people and all while I got to be true to myself. And you know the best bit? They got to be them too. And that's where this business came from, formerly Branding by Nicki. Ugh, that name still makes me feel a bit sick. I remember coming up with it two days before launch because I'd not checked out if the name The B Studio was available on social media, to have a short, sharp, shock when I found I couldn't have it. Well Nicki, just say it how it is on the tin (practising my own advice) and there was the name. Hmmm... funny how it's easy to help others but you can royally screw it up for yourself. But more about that later.

It still wasn't always easy. I wasn't born to do this. I've never been surrounded by business people, so it was a whole new world to me being an entrepreneur and I think even though I knew I could brand the hell out of a business woman, it's been a long road and a lot of being a bit of a follower and a sheep to get me to where I am writing this right now.

I'd be the one spending day after day, scrolling through social media, seeing what everyone else was doing and trying to put my own twist on it, or creating my own version. I mean that is how people speak about branding, right? I can't suddenly have a different opinion. I didn't want to just learn from the best, and then mimic some other designer's business plan and put all their knowledge to waste. But I felt scared to be something different, scared to be something more. Scared to be the real me. The real experts out there were talking about it in a certain way so I should do the same. Right? Heaven forbid I stepped out of turn and got told I was wrong. I knew that feeling too well.

But I knew I would never be running my business from a place of truth and I was never going to love it if I didn't change. So I decided to throw out the rule book. Who said I couldn't talk about building a brand differently? Who said I only had to talk about colours and logos and fonts? Who said I couldn't get people to think about their brand in a way they'd never considered? And who said that I couldn't share my opinions and use my voice, even though I was still finding it? Well the thing is... no one! No one said these things. The only person telling me this was me!

BECAUSE THERE IS NO A-Z BLUEPRINT FOR YOUR BUSINESS

No guide that fits you into a set style or sticks you into a strategic formula. We might think there is. But what happens if that blueprint doesn't work for you? What about if you want something different and you want to play by your own rules? Find your own lane. Be your own person.

It's probably only been in the last year or so and with the help of some phenomenal business women and their support that I've become the woman I am today. It's amazing the difference a supportive community makes. And when I think back, the woman I am today has been there all along. Betty could see it and now I can see it too. I can see a clear path. A place in the brand market that's missing what I have to say. And by stepping into my superpower and shouting from the rooftops about why I am the one to show women how to brand themselves, others now see it as well. So it goes to show that there will always be bumps in the road and no matter what happens to you on your journey it all happens for a reason. It's all a lesson, a teaching, an experience and it gets you to the point you are at today.

But what about you? How is this relevant for you as a business woman, reading this book, right now?

I bet if you were in front of me right now, I could see some of this in you. Maybe not quite the same journey but I see these traits in so many business women that are just like you, like me. And how do I know? Because you wouldn't be picking up this book to find out how you can run your business and attract your clients by flipping it and being a little more you and a lot less them, if you weren't doing the same. Because every single day, I see women falling into the trap of being a mould of something they think is going to work.

FIND YOUR
OWN LANE.
BE YOUR OWN
PERSON.

———

So when I talk about my story and the fact that little girls should be seen and not heard, well, it's turned into something completely different now. Whereby people that don't fit into a certain "framework" are also being told to be a certain way, act a certain way and to not voice their opinions. And it doesn't have to be abusive or nasty. It's what we take in day to day, subconsciously. From the media, on social media, our friends, you name it. But are we really being told this? Nobody made a rule book for how to be a good woman - or did they? So maybe we are not being told it, but just thinking it's how we have to be. To not showcase anything that is just pure amazeballs about us.

And I want you to think right now... is this right? Have you noticed yourself doing this? Feeling this way?

Now this isn't just in our business lives. This can be in our personal lives too. I bet there has been some point in your life at some stage, when you've been put down, told you are wrong, made to think a certain way or even believed you had to be a certain way. And it's stuck with you, right?

Where you hid as the woman you wanted to be and followed that stereotypical path that was set out for you. Designed for you. Perhaps it was following the 9-5 path: you know the one I mean, where we climb the ladder and strive and reach for the next step, even if it doesn't set your soul on fire. Or being a good housewife and Mum, and as much as you love it, you sit there wondering when there will be a time for you.

Let me introduce the amazing Lisa Hawkyard to you. I remember my very first call with her. I was absolutely petrified as I knew she was the Mum to a very well-known singer so I don't know why but I thought she would be very far off the lovely, smiley faced woman I was greeted by. You see, Lisa has spent all her life looking after others, being the Mum, the wife, the driving instructor, the home maker and even though at the time she came to me she had a brand identity in place, it was no reflection of who she truly was and it didn't say what she actually wanted to say. Lisa decided it was time to make a change, it was time to be the person she was destined to be and she wanted to stop playing small. She wanted to put herself first.

She wanted to attract other women who'd stopped themselves from being who they truly wanted to be and empower them to do it bloody differently. And the best bit? As a mindset coach there are so many dos and don'ts. So many ways to teach the tools of the trade, it's like a rule book. You have to have all your shit together, you have to have dealt with all the shit you've been dealt. But Lisa wasn't perfect, and of course she still had wobbles. And what I love most about Lisa is that she shared them. She wasn't a robot and she'd tell her audience that. It was about building a brand with integrity and heart. It was about showcasing who she really was.

One of my favourite conversations was her being so nervous to tell me that she wanted to add some "woo" into the copy on her website because she truly believed in it. I guess the scary bit was admitting that she wanted to talk about asking the universe for things when so many people are anti-woo. Would it put people off? Maybe... but who cares? And you can guess my reaction? "Do it! Why on earth shouldn't you?" Because it was her, it was her belief and you shouldn't hide any part of that. It was amazing seeing Lisa's results, seeing her confidence in herself when she could finally take down that barrier, stop being who she thought she had to be and started being who she wanted to be. Saying what she wanted to say, running her business HER way. See, all that actually needed to happen was that someone needed to listen to her because she knew what she wanted but was being stifled. And since then she's had more enquiries than ever, she runs her business by her rules and she can be who she wants to be. She finally did something for herself and she didn't care what anyone else thought. It was her time.

Lisa Hawkyard,
lisahawkyardcoaching.com

It may be that you too have a story like Lisa's and it's time to do something for you. But I bet for most of you the thing that is stopping you from being true to who you are comes from the steps you have already started taking on your entrepreneurial journey. With the busy online world filled with business coaches, motivational speakers, all the experts around you telling you how to grow your business and you follow it one step, then the next step, and somewhere along the way you've lost who you are and feel you need to put on your facade of what a successful business woman acts like. You put on the mask of who you need to be as a woman to get ahead. And you lose some of what makes you, you in the meantime.

And I get it, because it's a busy world out there and more and more entrepreneurs pop up every day and unfortunately, we fall into a trap of either worrying people won't want to hear from us or being quiet for fear of saying the wrong thing or being judged. So we start to look and sound like everyone else because we know it works, well, for them anyway; it's going to be "easier" as we don't have to find our own way and we feel lost because we no longer know how to just show up to our audience as our true selves.

But imagine a world for a second where every single person thought, acted and spoke in the exact same way. All of those people that you admire and look up to. Imagine a world where everyone was scared to speak up and be passionate about what they really cared about and what their mission was. A world where people didn't help people because they weren't really being who they wanted to be. Not saying what they needed to say to the right people who needed to hear it. Who would we have to learn from? Who would we help? Who would we inspire? How would we stand out? And the thing is, all of these people that we are following and admiring have all learnt how to be the face of their business, how to win their audience over by being their brand.

And you know what? They've done it all their way. So we don't need to follow their path, we need to find our own. By all means listen, learn but it's about finding our own voice, our own journey, telling our own stories, making our own mistakes and learning from them. But showing our audience and potential customers that we are the ones for them. To attract them by being 100% unapologetically you. No airs, no graces, no similarities with our competitors. Just us. And that can't just be some pretty logos and a fancy website. It's more than that. It's about you. What makes you special. What makes you the go-to, non-negotiable person for your clients. It's about being the face of your brand. And your time is now.

03

BUT IT'S A BIT BLOOMIN' SCARY. AIN'T IT?

There was a reason I called this book (and my business) Just Brand You... and I bet by now you get the idea that for me and all of the women I work with that we threw away the rule book, we broke the stereotypes and we pulled down the fifty foot concrete wall that stopped us showing the true version of ourselves in our businesses and we just show up as who we are. But before I start telling you how to do that, we need to have a deep and honest discussion.

Because there is something stopping you from achieving your full potential. Something that will always stop you. And it's easy to say it's what someone said to you when you were young, or when you first started. Or spend all your days looking at everyone else and wondering how on earth you will ever get what they've got because you are telling yourself you are not good enough.

WE THREW AWAY THE
RULE BOOK. WE BROKE
THE STEREOTYPES AND
WE PULLED DOWN THE
FIFTY FOOT CONCRETE
WALL THAT STOPPED
US SHOWING THE TRUE
VERSION OF OURSELVES

That it's easy for them, and you are nothing special, right? That there is so much competition in your market that you just won't be seen? And even if you were seen then those clients would just pick the other people with more experience over you anyway? Yep! I can hear you RIGHT NOW! I can almost picture you, nodding along. But the thing is, there is only one person who can control all of those niggly feelings you get when I tell you that it's time to stop playing small and it's time to go out there as the face of your brand and that person, I am afraid to say, is you.

I am going to split this chapter into sections, because it's a biggie and for each of you reading this there might be a different thing that you fear or worry about when it comes to being the face of your brand. And for some of you it might be all of them; I know it was for me. But I promise you that if you can overcome some of these fears and stop thinking it's about you and start focusing on showing up, connecting with your audience and making a change in their world then you won't regret taking this step. And we can't push forward and build that strong brand we all strive for if we don't break down these barriers. Right now, it may feel scary but let's deep dive into these beliefs you are telling yourself about stepping out of your comfort zone and give them a swift kick up the backside once and for all.

Let's talk vulnerability

Probably one of the scariest and most understandable reasons as to why women do not want to put themselves at the centre of their business is feeling too vulnerable. I see it time and time again: another cheapy logo pushed out, the brand "sorted" and off you go into the big old entrepreneurial world thinking that ideal clients are just going to come streaming in, while you post photos of your products, work and the odd quote that sparks your fancy once a day on Instagram. But it's fine, because it looks great, right? And surely people are attracted to that? And it sure beats actually showing them who you truly are.

Then you hear yet another business coach, marketing guru or brand expert on the internet saying that it isn't enough, that you can no longer hide behind that beautiful feed and that it's time to show the f*ck up! And the panic sets in. It did for me too. But if I'd carried on as I was, I wouldn't be where I am today and I generally think my business would have fizzled out by now.

I remember when my first business coach told me I needed to be out there more, that I needed to show my face, get more visible and I honestly thought I'd vom on the spot. I am still not entirely sure why it was such a problem. It looked so easy watching everyone else do it and I'd spent my childhood on stages doing musical theatre. But I wonder if it was so scary because when you are on the stage, you are playing a character; it's like putting on a facade, pretending to be someone else. And although you know that behind the costumes, the make-up and the funny voices you are still there, it just didn't feel quite as daunting. But this was real life. This was me. I couldn't put on my pink lady jacket and start prancing around singing, "Look at me, I'm Sandra Dee." Firstly, because real life isn't like playing Rizzo in Grease and I think people would generally think I'd lost my marbles, and secondly, because no one wants to hear about keeping their filthy paws off my silky drawers.

BECAUSE REAL LIFE ISN'T LIKE PLAYING RIZZO IN GREASE

But no, seriously, all humour aside, it was a real issue for me. One of those nail-biting issues that at the time I thought was completely pathetic. And I really beat myself up about it. I mean, I'm not bungee-jumping into a cave or stepping into a boxing ring with Mike Tyson, am I? It's just a Facebook Live and a few brand photos. So why do I and so many women find it so intimidating? Well, for me, it all came down to "pretending" to be an expert. Because at the time that's what I truly believed I was doing. I found myself spending hours and hours looking at other people's live videos and wondering how on earth they sounded so confident, how they didn't muck up every five minutes and pause like a stuck record, going uhm, uhm, uhm, while slowly feeling more and more like a beef tomato! I mean, how does that gibbering mess sound like an expert? So I guess in the beginning I always hoped and prayed that I could stay hidden behind my own little safety net on the internet. And I want you to stop beating yourself up if this is the trap that you fall into at present, because I get it and let's face it, it's easier that way. It's comfortable. It's a great excuse.

So trust me when I say I understand how scary it is being the face of your brand. I had to give myself a proper talking to when I nervously shook my outstretched finger ready to press that live button and trust me, my first Facebook Live was horrendous. I did it in a group that I felt really comfortable in with some of the loveliest ladies but I still cancelled it halfway through. My Facebook Lives were so bad in the beginning that I gave myself a nervous blink. Not a little one, a million miles per hour nervous blink that could be seen from a mile off. I remember my friend texting me and asking if I'd developed a new facial tic. Not helpful!

But it isn't the actual Live that I think the problem is here for women. It's the fear of being judged. The fear that someone is going to call you out. The fear that someone is going to say, "Look at this woman banging on about her 'specialist subject' well... she's wrong!" It's about opening ourselves up to opinions and trusting in ourselves that we actually are the expert and that we do actually know what we are talking about. Or more to the point, believing we are the expert.

So let me tell you right now, that not everyone knows what you know! And not everyone can talk about it the same way you do. And even if you are talking about a similar subject, your audience might just need to hear it this one time more, but from you, for the penny to drop. And better yet, if you put your own twist on it, use your own examples, then NO ONE can tell you it's wrong. Because it's part of your lessons you've learnt on your journey. It's your experience. It's time to own it.

IN YOUR BRAND JOURNAL

I want you to go away today and think about all the things you truly want to say to your audience. The lessons you want to teach, the subjects you want to deliver and then journal around your own experiences with these subjects. This is called unique storytelling content and no one can take that away from you. And I will teach you how in Chapter Sixteen.

It's not you, it's them

We also have to remember that it isn't just about you! Do we honestly think our audience cares if we *uhm* all the time, or if we don't look directly into the camera or if we lose our train of thought and end up laughing our heads off mid-way through a Live? It's actually the complete opposite.

Let's remember here that people buy from people. Correction! People buy people. Read that again.

They buy from people they relate to. And not everyone likes a polished Pauline, sitting at her immaculate desk in her power suit and high heels with a perfect match to her brand colours. Some people want to see a real person. Someone who doesn't have all their sh*t together and who sometimes maybe, does muck it up a bit. Someone they feel is accessible, someone who feels achievable. There's a great fact about social media... *"Most social media channels are a place where people hang out with their friends and family, people they are interested in, so they are actually put off by the polished professional look and favour something more real."*

And the second you stop worrying about what you look like, or what you sound like or whether you pronounce every word correctly (jeez, I'd be out of business the number of times I make up new words on a Live), is the second you spend more time thinking about the value you are going to deliver and more time helping people. And when you help people and nurture people and show them who you really are, they are more likely to buy. Because not everyone knows what you know. Not everyone is inside your head and the knowledge that you have needs to get out there. Your stories, your experiences, your lessons. We never know who needs to hear it; we never know who is listening.

IN YOUR BRAND JOURNAL

Take all of those negative things you are telling yourself about being who you truly are and turn them on their heads. Write them all down, all the amazing reasons why people should hear from you. Live with them, read them, believe them.

Let's talk trolls

And no, I am not talking about the cool ones from back in the day with the fluorescent pink pointy hair. They are the only cool trolls. FACT. Also, can we just take a moment to talk about how terrible the new, reinvented, modern versions are. I mean, what is that? Don't mess with something that ain't broken. A lesson we should all learn when it comes to our brands.

What we are talking about here is internet trolls, or "keyboard warriors" as you may have heard them called. And I am not going to lie to you - when they come out from under their rickety wooden bridge and hit you with a big sucker punch, it's tough. But I don't like to think of them that way. I like to think of them as little jackpot leprechauns instead, as when you get them you know it's because you are halfway to being brand famous. Why? Because to get one of these pesky little blighters you must be everywhere. People are talking about you, you are nailing the social algorithms, and you have just the right amount of an opinion that you are putting some people off. And it might not feel like it when they are making their opinions about you "needing to brush your hair" or "lose some weight" (yep, I've had both of those) but trust me, it says a lot more about them than it does about you. And when you've branded correctly you will have a tribe of followers, ready with their pitchforks (hmmm that seems a bit violent), their pom poms ready to cheerlead that troll right out the park.

DON'T MESS

WITH SOMETHING THAT AIN'T BROKEN. A LESSON WE SHOULD ALL LEARN WHEN IT COMES TO OUR BRANDS.

———

I remember scrolling through Facebook once and seeing the most awful comments about a famous makeup artist. She'd brought out a new product and had demonstrations of what it would look like on a very attractive model and out they came, from under their bridges, ready to pounce. "This looks horrid." "Who actually thinks this looks good?" "She looked better before."... and the worst, "She doesn't even have any proper skills as a makeup artist."

The woman is world famous, so we all know that one isn't true and so what if it just isn't right for YOU but is for tonnes of others? Well, if that's the case, fine, scroll on by, my friend. Why can't people just do that? It always amazes me how shallow people can be to just not like something and *ignore* it. But you know the best bit? All these people did was boost the algorithm of her post. Facebook saw it as having more comments and pushed it out even further to others. And of course, the make-up artist handled it perfectly and killed all the nasty comments with kindness, celebrated all the amazing cheerleading ones and voila, tonnes more views.

I was given these wise words once by one of my best friends. "When someone says something nasty or mean to you, it is rarely a reflection of something you've done. If it was, they'd message you privately and speak to you about it. The type of person prepared to message publicly with their vile opinions are the people suffering themselves." I guess when you put it that way you almost have to feel sorry for these troll people and know that deep down there is a bigger reason than your hair not being brushed, for them to be giving their two penneth.

So we have to start thinking of trolls as good things. Leprechauns. Weird, I know! Because we don't want to appeal to every single person on the internet and I am going to talk to you about that a lot in the next chapter, and for good reason. It's one of the most crucial steps. I know it's hard but let's remember to think of the hundreds of people we can be helping to push forward, while our little leprechauns stay exactly where they are.

I'd rather be cruising down the fast lane.

Anyone who says they haven't suffered with imposter syndrome at some point in their life is fibbing. Fact. I still to this day have my own fears and worries when it comes to people I compare myself to. The difference is I have the tools now to not let it stop me. But what is imposter syndrome? Because when we know what it is, we know how to tackle it.

The dictionary definition for imposter syndrome is this: *Impostor syndrome is a psychological pattern in which an individual doubts their accomplishments and has a persistent internalized fear of being exposed as a "fraud".*

So you can understand why this isn't just something that happens to people when they are new to business, right? I bet I am not the only one who always focuses on the next thing to do, the next achievement, and spends very little time celebrating how well I've done, how far I've come. You with me? And one of the biggest things that holds us back in our businesses is that little imposter devil that sits on our shoulders, telling us we are not good enough. Telling us that, "we'll never be as good as Judy." But the truth is, it's only ourselves telling us these things. No one is actually sitting there saying *who the f*ck is she?* And the sad thing is that I see so many talented, amazing people stopping themselves from being the best they possibly can be because that imposter is louder than the other, much quieter inner voice, telling them that they can do it. You see, the devil will always win if we allow it. It will always be feared. Telling us not to do it, telling us to stop showing the real person behind the brand. And it's why imposter syndrome becomes one of the biggest reasons that women just like us don't grow their businesses.

It's easier to hide away, saying, "It's ok for them, they've got it all together," but the crazy thing is, I bet every single female battles with it. And even when you think you've beaten it and nailed it on the head, another little niggly voice comes in and tells you something different.

And it doesn't matter what stage you are at, what position you are in, all different levels of business are going to bring up their own little gremlins. Now, we can't make this go away completely today, but we can find tips and solutions on how to deal with it.

I want to tell you a story of when I started my brand business. Of a time when I spent tonnes of time comparing myself to every other brand designer on the internet... especially one! Let's call her Gemma. Gemma, on the outside, seemed to have it all. She was recommended all the time, people were talking about her, from the looks of her social media feeds she had tonnes of clients and then there was little old me, with loads of experience and tonnes of potential but I'd just started.

My coach had recommended me to an absolute dreamboat of a client and she would have been my first proper client, so there was a lot of pressure here, but she also recommended Gemma. Well, that was it, wasn't it? It was never going to happen. Gemma had all the testimonials, she was raved about, I might as well not even bother. I couldn't "compete" with that, and so the niggly little devils started telling me I wasn't good enough. However, the potential client asked to speak to both of us, we arranged a discovery call and to say I was nervous was an understatement, it meant so much. I showed up to this call a nervous wreck, already knowing I wasn't going to get the job. It was Gemma's, it had to be. And the woman kept me waiting and waiting to let me know if I'd sealed the deal. It was my worst nightmare.

Then, one day, I got an email ping through. "I'm really sorry Nicki but I've decided to go with another designer. As much as I thought you were lovely, I just felt that the other person had more experience and sounded more confident and I think she can serve me better on this occasion."

Of course she did. I showed up a quivering mess and Gemma probably turned on all the charm. Sold herself. You see, I'd already talked myself out of this job and I think in other circumstances, perhaps the client would have picked me. But I'd spent so long looking at how amazing Gemma was, that I forgot who I was.

It wasn't until I actively stopped following Gemma on social media and focused on my own stuff that things really changed for me. I am a firm believer that anything that triggers you in life and stops you from being the best version of yourself needs to go and she was one of them. What I didn't know was that Gemma also felt the same about the new kid on the block. Small world, really. See, we all have things that trigger us, we all have worries and concerns but we get to choose what we let in and what we don't. And we also have to realise that we live in a world of social media where it always seems like the grass is greener on the other side. Well, let me tell you, it isn't. We all have demons, all have wobbles, but if you picture three lanes of traffic, the first two jam packed with cars, all doing the same thing, all following the same trends and then you look at the third lane. The third lane is clear and wide open. That lane, if you choose to take it, gives you a special power. That lane has your name on it. It's your lane. Where competition isn't a thing anymore because you are so focused on your path, your journey, how you can be completely different. How you can be more you. It's time to take up that lane now. Ladies. It's time to stop looking at the Gemma's on the internet and start cruising in the fast lane.

IN YOUR BRAND JOURNAL

There is no quick fix to solve imposter syndrome, no one-stop shop. But what you need to start thinking about is, what are your strengths? What can you showcase to the world? What are your gifts and your talents and what is stopping you from using them? Then think about who told you the opposite. Because I guarantee that person who told you that is yourself. And it takes time to change our thought patterns of how we think of ourselves, time to change these beliefs. But if we keep our eye on the prize, we focus on our own lane and stop worrying about everyone else's, well, that's when the magic happens.

I've got 49,999 problems but my brand ain't one

I always ask my audience how they are feeling, how can I help them, how can I support them in the best way possible. And I did this right before a launch in February 2020. See I wanted to use their language, to describe how they feel, because let's face it half the time people don't even know they need you. One of my favourite things that came out of this was someone saying, "I am trying absolutely everything and I still feel like I have 50,000 tabs open in my brain." Cor! That's a lot of tabs. I don't know about you, but I struggle even sitting at my desk and looking at my computer screen if there is too much going on. That complete and utter feeling of overwhelm of what to do next. Our brains are exactly the same. One of the most common reasons that people don't build a successful brand is because they are concerned that it's another thing on the to-do list and they worry that building a brand won't solve all their problems.

I get it: there are much shinier things out there on the internet, things that make you cash fast, grow your audience quickly, position you as the expert. And I've been right there, investing in one thing, then another thing, hoping it is going to turn everything around. Feeling like my head is going to explode with the lives, the social media, the audience building, the sales calls, the admin... the list goes on. The problem here, ladies, is that all those people you admire and look up to, with their successful businesses, have a brand. Whether they think they do or not, they are all where they are right now because of not just a solid business strategy but also a bloomin' great brand.

There's an amazing quote by Jeff Bezos, CEO at Amazon: *"Your brand is what people say about you when you are not in the room."* See, building that rock solid brand is all about reputation, it's about how people connect with you, and in turn buy from you. But for some reason, people place it at the bottom of their to-do list because it isn't a quick fix. And nor should it be. When you get it right, when you pull down all those barriers stopping you from stepping into your superpower and becoming the woman that you are meant to be and you stop putting on a facade, stop the comparing, stop worrying about everyone else and you just start to truly show up as the real you, you can close 49,999 other tabs and solely focus on one. You. See, we don't need bells and whistles, we don't need to be told who we can and can't be and we can see all these amazing things on the internet that grow our businesses and we can action them. Why? Because we can put our twist on them, play by our own rules, have complete and utter clarity and, most importantly, know that we can do it with strength, to get the results we want. We can do it our way. Let me show you...

04

I WANT YOU TO CULL YOUR AUDIENCE

DISCLAIMER!

You can have more than one ideal client! There are two ways to niche:

1. on your ideal client;
2. on how you are different from everyone else out there.

By the end of this chapter and the next you will know how to niche effectively and which one suits you and your business. NOTE: There are no rules and in fact I encourage you to break them and do what is right for you.

Ideal client is a mad one, right? And I bet you've heard it a million times on the internet where coaches say you need to understand your ideal client and they send you off on a quest to find out all about them. You know, where they live, what clothes they buy, what they had for dinner last night. I can't tell you the number of times I've had clients so confused about what and who their ideal clients are. I think there are two camps of people when it comes to identifying them.

1. The person who knows everything about them but has no idea what to do with it... and are left feeling that it was a completely pointless task, but they give themself a brownie point anyway because they've ticked something off the never-ending to-do list created for them by every other coach on the internet.

2. And my favourite one, the person who says they have no ideal client at all and that they would get much further along if they just appealed to everyone, talked to everyone... and tries desperately to attract everyone.

Well, let me tell you, ladies, neither are going to benefit you, because if you don't know how to use all of this information or worse, you brush it under the carpet and save the task for a rainy day, then you will end up attracting no one.

Now I get it, no matter what camp you fall into. I am going to explain right now how it all works, so grab a brew, get that pen out, because we are about to start our learning. Let's start with the easiest one...

If I put something out there for everyone I will make more dollar

This is where I started. Let me take you back to when I had my stationery business. I'd never been an entrepreneur before. There was nobody in my family who'd done it either so I was pretty clueless. I remember sitting there for a good three months designing stationery suite after stationery suite, artwork after artwork and throwing half of it in the bin because it just wasn't good enough. Why do we do that to ourselves? Why do we never think anything we do is good enough? But that's beside the point... I'd finally settled on my final suites, designed my logo, crafted my website and set a launch date. I was all set. The day before I was due to go live, I set up my social channels, followed a few industry people, and popped out a launch post saying "I'm heeeerrre! Come buy from me." Now, I don't know what I expected: a rush of orders, a tonne of new likes, an overwhelming number of new followers, or what, but it couldn't have been any further from the truth. What I did get was crickets. Not even crickets, at least that would have made a bit of a buzz. No, no, what I got was complete and utter silence.

I'd love to say that this was just because I launched terribly (more about that in chapter fifteen), but this carried on for a good two months. My engagement went up on social, I started gaining new followers, but no one, not ONE person was buying. It was really disheartening. I can't tell you how many times I nearly burst into tears when someone asked, "Have you got an order yet?" No, no, I haven't got an order and do you honestly think I wouldn't tell you if I had? That I wouldn't be doing a crazy happy dance up and down my living room and ringing you up screaming down the phone, *"I've done it!"*

I sound really ungrateful here and it's not really their fault, they were just taking an interest, but I hated that it hadn't taken off instantly. I felt a bit of a failure. I doubted whether I was good enough. I started looking at everyone else and those niggly demons reared their ugly little heads. My stuff was just as good as others in the industry so why were they putting out client work after client work and I just kept shooting the same stationery suites I'd designed back when I started but all shot in different ways, with different backdrops and STILL got nothing! I just couldn't get my head around it.

Then I heard all about this thing called ideal client, the dream customer and how you couldn't appeal to everyone, you had to niche down to attract more clients. Sorry? I just didn't get it. How could attracting fewer people bring me more of them? Well, let me tell you, if I knew then, what I know now, I'd have got booked out a damn site quicker. You see, the reason we are told to niche down to attract more clients is because our audience are forever scrolling and scrolling through social media, looking for the perfect person. They are looking for someone who can produce what they want. What they need. But our audience need to hear from us or see us 27 times (it will probably be a hundred by the time I finish writing this book - it goes up every five minutes) before they are prepared to buy from us. So my idea of having six different stationery suites, appealing to every type of wedding just caused confusion.

There's a great quote by Donald Millar and he says: *"People are drawn towards clarity and away from confusion."* It sounds so simple, doesn't it, and it makes perfect sense. If you are doing a bit of stalking one day and see the stationery set of your dreams and the next set is some grungy, urban set that looks better placed in an abandoned warehouse than your posh country barn, then you are quickly going to think that the designer behind it isn't the person for you. And off you hunt for someone that is for you. And the designer is not getting you back after that. You're gone!

The second I realised I was trying to appeal to too many people, I concentrated on purely urban, edgy weddings and created stationery collections with a twist, for the couples who wanted something really standout and different. And guess what? My business soared. Five months later, I left my 9-5, was inundated with bookings and all with absolutely perfect clients. My social following grew even bigger, I started getting noticed and industry people such as top wedding plan-ners suddenly wanted to work with me. It seems like such a simple thing to change, just focusing on what you are best at, yet I'd spent two months beating myself up for not being good enough.

So how does this work for you?

How do we work this out? Well, it's simple really. Your ideal client is someone who you make up in your head. A dream person that you'd just love to work with. So stop overcomplicating it. This is probably one of my best teachings in this entire book. Because you know that person in scenario one who doesn't have a bloomin' clue what to do with their ideal client and how to work it out because they've never had an ideal client? Well, bingo! I've just told you what you need to do... make it up! There is no analysis that needs to be done at this point, no market research because let's face it - when you start out or you are relatively new, you haven't got a market to ask.

YOUR IDEAL CLIENT

IS SOMEONE YOU MAKE UP IN YOUR HEAD. A DREAM PERSON THAT YOU'D JUST LOVE TO WORK WITH.

SO STOP OVERCOMPLICATING IT!

———

Now there are two things we need to do when we work out our ideal client. When you break it down and you work through these steps, you are going to find it really simple... I promise!

Step one, the fun part. It's about understanding your ideal client like your best friend, probably the most common way you've heard about it on the internet. This is where you start to really visualise them, give them a name, really picture them. You are thinking about the brands they like, the places they shop, where they go on holiday, you name it! And you know your best pal, who tells you absolutely everything and you spend all the time in the world nattering to on the phone, painting each other's nails and going for boozy shopping trips... well, you need to know them better than her. And don't forget, it's really common for your ideal client to be a variation of yourself at a different time of your life.

As an example: One of my ideal clients (yep, I have more than one), the person who would buy my group program, is me, when I started out. They have tonnes of ambition, are super driven and know that when they first get that whiff of success that they'd stop buying handbags from Primarché and get themselves a Mulberry. But not just that. They want to help people. They know they have more to give.

So how do you really know your ideal client as a best pal?

To make it easy I've popped a few questions to ask yourself. I find that some people like to just answer the questions, get it all out and others still find that really hard to visualise. So another way is to answer all of these questions by getting out the magazines, heading over to Pinterest and doing it visually. Remember, there is no right or wrong here, it's about whoever you want to serve. Have fun... get creative, enjoy the process.

IN YOUR BRAND JOURNAL

You are not just looking for a short excerpt here or ten pins. I want you to be able to rabbit on to me about them for half an hour. Tell me EVERYTHING.

What is their name?
What age are they?
What gender?
What is their family situation like?
What does their house look like?
What are their favourite colours?
Where do they buy clothes?
What do they read? (magazines, books, blogs, websites)
Who inspires them?

Where do they find inspiration?
What are their favourite brands?
What is most important to them?
Do they paint their nails?
What style of clothing do they wear?
Who are their fave celebs?
What are their values?
What do they do in their spare time?
What music do they like?
What films do they like?
Do they watch tv? If so what type?
What are their passions? Is there something
that gets them on their soapbox?
What colours don't they like?
Is there anything that completely turns
them off?
Do they love animals?
Have they got a family?
What means the most to them in the entire
world?
What do they do in their free time?
What is this person's annual income?
What type of work does this person do?
Where or what was the last vacation and why
did this person love it so much?
What brand or product has so changed this
person's life that he/she now could not live
without it, and why?

Why do they need you?

The second thing we need to understand about our ideal client, which is nearly always missed, is what their struggles are. Why do they need you? It always amazes me when I ask this question and people start to flounder. They know what they offer but they don't know why their clients need it. And we must remember that our ideal client doesn't always know why they need us.

As an example, for my last launch I did a survey to my current audience asking them questions about what their biggest struggles were in their business, what their dream business scenario would be and if I had a magic wand what would change for them in their business. You'd be amazed at how many people felt completely lost when it came to pushing their businesses forward. I got some incredible insights and it was mad because none of it was related to building a brand. Why? Well, because it was then my job to educate them about the power a brand could have for them. One of the best lines I had from the survey was that they felt like they had 50,000 tabs open in their brain. So my entire campaign for the launch of my group program was about keeping just one tab open and closing 49,999 others and the only way you could do that was if you were rock solid with your brand. If you had the confidence to do all the things you needed to do to push your business forward and felt empowered to do these things just as the woman you are. That you needed to be the face of your brand. So by using this one line I had a huge increase in sales because I was telling them what they needed to hear. I was listening.

I mean, how can we serve our clients if we don't know their struggles? There are a million and one people out there who probably do what you do, but they might not be talking to their audience in the same way you can. They might be just putting out generic old copy that they think their audience wants to hear. Or worse, forever putting out Selly Sally posts, which is enough to turn anyone off. But you are going to start really thinking outside the box. You are going to say what they really need to hear.

IN YOUR BRAND JOURNAL

It's time to work out those pain points. It's ok to just list what they are if you know but if you are lucky enough to have an audience then you can directly ask them. Some examples of things to think about:

What are your clients' goals?
What are they struggling with?
Where do they want to be/What is their dream situation?
What is the situation now?

Why do they need to start this journey with
you? How are they feeling?
What transformation do they want? What
change do they need to see?

So now we know what they want to achieve, we need to
know what they are scared of. What stops them getting
to those goals? What stops them getting that dream
scenario? We forget that part of our brain protects us
from getting burnt and that part is usually the reason
why people don't get as far as the checkout with you.
They fear you won't have the magic solution, they fear
it won't work out, they fear you can't help them. So the
best people are talking to their ideal client's pain points
but also resonating with their fears and worries. If you
think of it, it's a little like I did in chapter three. I
showed you examples, times in my life, that I've experienced some of the things you've been through. It helps
you to know that I understand how it feels. It's not just
as easy as telling people the benefits, we have to discuss
their fears towards taking that leap. Towards that
change in themselves, whatever that may be.

IN YOUR BRAND JOURNAL

Think about the things stopping your clients. What is holding them back? What are they telling themselves? What have they experienced? Why do they feel they can't do this?

How do you use this information?

So here is where the true magic happens. I am going to tell you the secret they all don't want you to know until you pay them to tell you... How to actually use this information. How do we actually attract our ideal clients by knowing all of this? I told you that it's not just going to be one of those books where you do the work and park it, still feeling just as confused as when you picked it up. Because it's easy when you know how. Suddenly you can get in front of them, relate to them and show them that you get it! You can talk to them in a way others can't, and without these foundations it doesn't matter how pretty or epic or statement your brand is, they ain't gonna buy. So how does this work...

1. **Who they are as a person:** This is how you make sure your visuals attract them. There is absolutely no point, if your audience loves a bit of Mulbz, to be designing a brand that looks a little more Tesco F&F. And that is NOT me

slating F&F. Tesco's is where you buy your best clothes and I am not afraid to say I wander the clothes aisle when I head for the weekly shop. But my point is, you don't use this information for fun. It's to be able to know what style they are attracted to, how the brands they love talk, what colours they like. Because if we can understand the person, we can create visuals that attract them. Are they really into fashion? Great, let's look at fashion brands for inspiration and direction for our own brand. Do they read Cosmo rather than Tatler? Great, they love chatty conversations and a more friendly approach.

2. **Their pain points and transformations:** This is the fun bit. No one can talk to their ideal client if they don't know what they are struggling with and where they want to be. All of this information you gather gets used for your message, your web copy, your social posts, sales pages, the lot. It's our job to show them that what they need or are struggling with can be resolved with what we offer.

Don't think it works? Let me tell you about Nicky. No, not this Nicki, Nicky Booton from Nicky Booton Coaching. This woman is an absolute angel, with the kindest heart but the soul of a lioness. Nicky was on my very first

100% Brand You course and she just lit up every session. She was one of those people you just knew was going to be successful. She was doing it all in the right way, she cared about people deeply and the money was a byproduct of the results of that caring.

But Nicky had a problem. She was trying to attract every woman out there. Anyone who needed help with their mindset. Now, she'd been the cliche entrepreneur (sorry Nicky), following everyone on the internet saying *build an audience, start a group, nurture them,* but what Nicky hadn't realised is that it is really, really hard to attract every man and his dog into a Facebook group. Well, who are they associating with if they join? What are you going to help them with if the general feel is mindset in any form? Won't the majority of the content not be relevant for them? So it's safe to say that Nicky struggled to get her clients and struggled to grow that group, even though Nicky was insanely talented and epic at what she did.

It's understandable, really, if people don't feel spoken to. Why would they bother listening? See, the thing is, it's impossible to speak to that many people who have nothing in common with each other. And you will remember at the beginning of the chapter about my disclaimer about more than one ideal client and that is true, but they still have to have an interlinking commonality. Otherwise, you continue to alienate people with everything you put out there. You confuse them. So, I remember the best conversation with Nicky when she decided to niche down her ideal client and grow some balls and cull her audience in half.

It was scary. Her current small audience was about to get even smaller because it was no longer right for half the people there. But the results were phenomenal. Nicky now spends all her time speaking to female entrepreneurs who need help to reach their full potential. Her testimonials are just ace and the results she gets for people is amazing. And that's all she's ever wanted. To help. She can achieve her mission. And why is she suddenly booking clients? Well, it's because she is speaking directly to them. Talking to their pain points, understanding and relating to their problems and better yet, with that, her audience grew, her client lists grew and Nicky finally feels like she is making a difference in the world.

Nicky Booton,
nickybootoncoaching.co.uk

You see, it may seem scary, the idea of culling your audience, but by niching down, it's highly likely that your sales will go up. I am not saying you only have to speak to one person on their own, because that would be a lie. I am not saying that this is a cookie cutter approach whereby you speak to one person and niche on that. But imagine the clarity with everything you do when you finally just have one type of person to speak to, and it's that dream client you worked on in the beginning. But now you are attracting other like-minded individuals too and they love you, they think you are ace and you are getting results in your business finally. And you know how that feels? Bloomin' marvellous.

Now, remember all of these pain points and transformations from this chapter. Keep them safe, because you are going to need them for what's next. I am super excited...

05

DON'T JUST SAY IT.
LIVE IT.

A nice little short and to the point chapter that quite frankly couldn't fit anywhere else but is so crucial to total brand domination that it had to be included. Okay, maybe that is a bit extreme and no domination will actually happen but it is really crucial not just to brand success but also for our own peace of mind and the alignment of our brands.

I want to talk to you all about what you stand for and what values are non-negotiable for you. We've all heard the well-known saying that people buy from people, right? But it's bigger than them just liking your personality. They have to love and connect with what you stand for. Now, this is something that sometimes I've been accused of being a bit ranty pants about. I've seen people again and again identify their key non-negotiable values and then go out there shouting them from the rooftops. I am really honest; I am super authentic; I'm really loyal; I am trustworthy. But then when it comes down to it and people follow you or buy from you, some of those values just don't seem as true as you'd like to believe. And it makes me sad because I see it all far too often and actually, we shouldn't just be saying our values, we should be living by them too.

I can't even stress how important it is to identify your brand values, because they are the stepping-stone to help you with who you want to attract (because, top tip, they will share your values) but even more importantly who you will want to learn from as your business grows. I kid you not, there is nothing that gets me more soapboxy than people who don't align with my values. It's like a trigger point and I know it is for many. Have you ever found yourself really annoyed when a friend has done something you just categorically don't believe in? THAT is because your values have been broken. They've not aligned to something you feel so passionately about. So I choose to surround myself with people who align to mine, whether that be business collaborations, my clients or my coaches that I invest in. You notice that more and more of these people think very similarly to you, they will act very similarly to you and they will believe in all the same things you do.

That doesn't mean we all have to agree. What a boring world that would be. But you notice that you are at your most comfortable when you are surrounded by people who share the same beliefs as you. And your clients will be the same. It's a busy old world out there and you are going to find lots of people who don't have the values you do and that is okay, they are not your people. It doesn't make them bad people. They are just not for you.

Our values define us. They make us the brand we truly are. And more often than not, second to the results we get, it's our values that get people talking about us when we are not in the room. Now, no-one likes being spoken about when they are not there but if you have nothing to hide, you are true to yourself and you build a brand that is 100% aligned to who you are, then they will ONLY be speaking about the things you want them to speak about when you are not there to do it yourself.

So how do we find our brand values?

Well, a lot of the time it comes down to what you believe. I mean you can just google a list of brand values and you need to weed those down to a core five at least. Five that you abide by. Jeez, I sound like I am writing the law. But it is so true. And a lot of the time when I work with my clients or even when I do this work for myself, I manage to get it down to fifteen and then I am stuck. And I remember one of my incredible mindset coaches saying to me, *but they aren't non-negotiable.* That's just what you like the idea of and hope to live up to. But when you find your true top five, these are things you just couldn't live without. If we didn't have them we would really struggle, feel betrayed, be really upset or annoyed and just feel damn right uncomfortable.

So here are mine: Honesty, loyalty, respect, authenticity (although I hate that word now everyone uses it) and creativity.

And I honestly do live by them. I don't need to shout them from the rooftops every day, I just show them. I won't ever lie. I tried when I was a kid with some little white lies to get me out of trouble and I just giggled hysterically. Once you have my love, I am fiercely loyal and will put you before anything for myself. I offer the utmost respect for people but I can lose it quickly if it's not returned. I couldn't be any more myself if I tried as I honestly can't be arsed to be anything else (what an effort) and that formed an awful lot of why I do what I do. To help others to be the same. And finally, creativity, because if you took that away from me I think I would crumble. It's my outlet.

Now don't get me wrong, I am not saying you can't stand there saying your values. Of course you can and who am I to tell you what you can and can't say anyway, but what you CAN'T do and I mean CAN'T is say that you are your value and go and do the polar opposite, because that loses brand respect. It gives your clients a reason not to trust you and when your client loses trust in you it's really hard to get that back.

IN YOUR BRAND JOURNAL

So what are your non-negotiable things? What do you stand for? What can't you live without? Take some time to think about that.

06

IT AIN'T WHAT YOU DO, IT'S THE WAY THAT YOU DO IT.

To the change makers
The bold, strategic action takers
The visionaries and the dreamers

Your time is now.

Time to spark change
To overcome challenges,
And to do it all, together

Time to do it your way
To always stay true to what makes you, you
And what makes you shine

Time to make your impact
With fun, with kindness
And with the energy to never give up

Your superpower is yours to own
The world is yours to change

It's time to create your legacy

Boom! What an inspiring manifesto, right? Where do I sign up? I wanted to start this chapter a bit differently, by introducing you to one of my lovely clients, Lisa Wynn. An epic force with a big mission... to help women to change the world. And a bit of sass added in for good measure. The perfect martini cocktail if I may go so far to say... shaken of course, never stirred. I still remember our first call, when I saw a side to Lisa I'd never seen before.

You see, I am relatively intuitive. I see spark in people and can easily see who they truly are. It's why I am so passionate about helping women to be the face of their brands. But I will never just tell a woman the answer. They need to find it on their own. That's when the true lightbulb moments come. But Lisa wasn't going to be like every other woman. Normally I receive a slight kick back to my methods because they sometimes push you a little bit too hard, but it's always followed by a realisation that actually they can be whoever they damn want to be.

But not Lisa. From our first call I knew she had a fire I'd never seen before, but she was trapped in a brand that didn't convey everything that was just incredible about her. So on our first call, as I pushed and pulled and poked and prodded to find out exactly what made Lisa, Lisa, I got greeted with a hand slam on the table, followed by just a few tears and a, "I don't have an ideal client and I won't ever have one. Who am I to tell a woman they can't change the world and why do I have to fit into these rules of what coaches teach?"

Well, I was put in my place and for the next six weeks I'd say we continued on that roller coaster.

But this was probably one of my most exciting yet challenging projects to date. Because finding what made this powerhouse different and watching her transformations daily was just next level for me. The clarity that I saw as part of this change, when she could clearly communicate what it was she set out to do without having to follow any rules and saying exactly what she wanted to say, was immense. She called it a "creative soup." And with that soup came a side of confidence. She was so excited about the work we did together that she started talking about it and the more she spoke about it the stronger it became. And within just a few weeks she made 4x the original investment she'd made in working with me. And we'd not even put her brand out there by that point. Not bad for a can of Campbell's, right?

You see, I am telling you this for a reason. Because sometimes this is one of the most crucial things that people miss when they talk about building a brand. No logo or website will give you that level of clarity.

And both you and your clients need that to get the results, secure the deal and move forward.

I want to paint you a picture so you can start to visualise how this plays out for you... You know that really annoying feeling when you're stuck in stand-still traffic and it feels like you've been stuck there for days and you just can't see the light at the end of the tunnel? You know the one I mean... I seem to always end up in that situation when we do a big drive up North after work at 8pm on a Friday night and I am utterly shattered. The worst time to travel. And I must admit I don't have the best patience. I need a magic carpet. I am still slightly unsure why my life isn't a bit more like a fairy tale and why Aladdin hasn't shown up yet. But enough of that dream... we've got business to do.

You see, that traffic jam we've all painfully sat in is exactly what it's like in our business. We spend so much time stuck in a clogged up world of comparing ourselves to everyone else. Especially people that do exactly what we do. But it doesn't have to be the case. Imagine if that never happened again? Imagine the feeling of having a completely separate lane that only you are allowed to drive in. It's the untouchable lane and if anyone sets foot in it, you don't even waver because you know you are a million miles ahead of them. You put the car into fifth gear (or sixth if you are lucky) and you cruise down the motorway, taking in all of the scenery around you and you feel slightly smug. Why? Because you look over your left shoulder and you see for miles and miles the heavy traffic behind you and you just can't imagine how you ever lived your life queuing in those lanes before. How you ever woke up every day in your business trying to fit into someone else's box.

Because it's time we found our own lane for our business. A place where no matter what happens we don't have to be continually fighting like Rocky Balboa to get our clients' attention and we finally start celebrating who we are and what makes us special. A place where we never have to look back again. But it's not always easy and for some reason it's something we all struggle with when we start out as entrepreneurs. I don't know if it is because we are all stereotypically British (although my overseas friends seem to struggle with this too), or maybe because we are women and we have been conditioned to not shout about how amazing we are and to just shut the hell up and get on with it, but we can't ever shout about what makes us special.

But to get ahead in this crazy world as an entrepreneur, we need to know who we are and what we bring to the table. And when I say this, I definitely don't mean that top level statement. You know that 'I am a brand designer' statement that ends right there with the biggest full stop at the end, because that's all you are comfortable saying. I don't just want to know what you do. I want to know why you do it. I want to know how you do it. And I want to know why I need it. And sometimes that means digging deep. And when you first start you might feel like there is a fifty foot wall stopping you from the realisation that you know is going to change your life. But if you don't know what transformation and benefit you are going to give me then why the hell should I?

Because let's just remember for a second how many others there are out there who do the same as us. How many others call themselves brand designers? And most importantly, how many others put that big giant f*ck off full stop at the end of it? So imagine your clients' overwhelm when looking for someone to create that pretty little logo and we are all out there saying the same thing. But then... along comes Sienna and Sienna speaks a bit differently, Sienna shows passion, Sienna speaks in a way no one else can. Sienna makes them suddenly get it. Well, I want to tell you a secret right here, right now: we can all be Sienna. Because there is only one you. Only you can say things in a way that you do, only you can bring the fire that you bring and it's time to start embracing it.

I am going to say this clear and simple once more. You. Are. You. Only you can be you. So it's time to stop struggling to show that to the world. It's time to stop struggling to see what is inside us. It's time we start.

So how do we start?

The first thing is, no matter where you are in business, to sit down and check in with yourself about whether the words coming out of your mouth when someone asks you what you do truly reflect what you are actually trying to achieve. But most importantly not to beat yourself up if you realise you have more to give but you are not showing it right now. We've all been there.

Late last year I had this exact realisation for myself, because it's easy telling people how to do it but doing it for yourself is another ball game. And unfortunately I don't have another me sitting there pulling it out of me like I want to do for women. For a good few months I had felt like I was underneath a ceiling. Like I was stopping myself from being who I truly wanted to be. Saying what I truly wanted to say. Whether that was fear, failure or who knows what, something was stopping me. I was holding myself back from showing the world my true potential. And I couldn't keep living that way. I've got a mission and just like my friend Lisa Wynn at the beginning of this chapter I had to get it out there. I couldn't continue not showing my clients how I could serve them like no other woman, because it was my duty to woman up and do it.

And I walked myself through this exact process that I am about to walk you through and had some huge realisation moments that led to some big changes in my business, including getting rid of a four thousand member Facebook group and changing it up for a community that truly spoke to what I wanted to portray.

So let's do this, shall we?

What are you trying to achieve?

How many times do you actually sit down with a pen and paper and ask yourself, "What do I want to achieve? What impact do I want to have in my industry? What impact do I want to have on my clients? What am I so passionate about in what I do? And how can I bring that passion to the surface?"

What is your why? Because you can't carry on with your blinkers on, guys. If you want to have impact, if you want to get known for what you do, then these questions must be answered. And there need to be streams of notes. Not one or two sentences, it's about allowing yourself that space to check in with yourself. Why you?

What is your X Factor or your secret sauce? It's a bit like the KFC secret blend. We all know there is a reason why we all love that finger-licking-good chicken but the Colonel knows it's his little bit of spice that makes him untouchable. So what is yours? What's your little bit of spice?

It could be as simple as the personality you bring to the table or the techniques you use, the way you say something, or the small number of people that you talk to, but somehow we've got to niche down here. We've got to stand out in a market that is ready to suck us all in and swallow us whole if we don't find a way to make ourselves different.

Does this business set our soul on fire?

You see, having a business isn't always sunshine and roses. So we have to be doing something we are passionate about and I can't tell you how many of my clients have lost their way doing what they think they should be doing rather than what they actually want to be doing. So we have to find what fuels that fire in your belly. What makes you wake up at 6am on a Monday morning and not think, "not another Monday." Where does that huge passion come from that took you from the safety net of a 9-5 into this entrepreneurial minefield where sometimes it can feel like you are strutting around with the peacocks in order to get seen, all trying to ruffle their feathers in the most attractive way? But we don't want to be a peacock.

We want to be seen for our talents, the difference we make and our skills, and we want to be able to shout about those instead. So what are you seeing in your industry day in and day out that you want to make different? What do you think needs to change? How are you going to improve it? Because this is where we start to see that spark in you. It's when the passion comes out and you stop hiding behind a rock. So the only ONE time I ask you to look at what others are doing is right now. But not to compare, not to make yourself feel shitty because what they are portraying looks a damn sight better than where you are at. But because it's time you start to see what needs to change.

What's the vision?

I remember the first time someone asked me what my why was. I remember fumbling around trying to come up with words that explained why I thought women needed a brand. Back in the day when I first started, it was all about visual representation. It was because they needed graphics that looked nice that they could use on their websites and social media... But that didn't get me excited. Yes, it was an excuse to use my creativity and skills but it's not the sort of thing that has me feeling giddy and a bit sick with those nervous butter-flies. You know, like that feeling when you are first in a relationship and you are getting ready for the third date? It couldn't just be about that for me. I had more vision than that. I knew I had more in me than that.

So I had to get deep down, nitty gritty, with my vision for what I wanted this business to achieve. What was my reason for doing this? And I am not talking about my personal reason why. Of course I want to provide a better life for my family, I want freedom, I want success, but my real reason why is you. Women just like you reading this. Women who give me the chance to fulfil my true vision. To empower women to unlock their full potential by being true to who they are. By empowering women just like you to have a voice, to be seen and heard, to feel powerful, to feel worthy.

Even tippity-tap typing these words out now puts a smile on my face. Because I know that step by step I am making my vision a reality. And it's all just the start. I have a purpose. And I believe, just as my Grandma Betty did, that I have a lot to give. So my business can't just be about money and the next financial milestone, it can't just be about my goals, it has to be about you too. And identifying these types of things are the things that make you stand out and see that spark. These are the things that make your client fall in love with you because they see it every day. They see the passion, they see your reasons and they see your why.

Now, let's check in for a second before you carry on. How many of you are sitting there saying, "I have no clue what my reason why is" and, "I don't have this huge mission that I want to achieve"? But I bet if you trust me right here and give yourself the time and ask yourself some of these questions, that you will find your vision. You will find your purpose. Because there is a reason we are doing this. It doesn't need to be to change the world, it doesn't need to be to change a life, but there is a vision. Even hairdressers have vision, they just communicate it right now as a service that all us ladies need - a good set of highlights and a blowdry - but actually they want to make women feel confident and great. You know that bouncy hair feeling when you walk out of a salon and feel a million dollars? Or a lady making candles is giving someone the time to light a candle, to take them back to a memory or a smell that they just adore and quietly the flames whisper *reeeellll-laaaaxxxx*. So it's not just about hair and candles anymore. And it's not just about logos and websites. It's about what those things do. The power they can have. No matter how big or small.

So spend some time, digging deep into why. Why are you doing this? Find that drive within you.

IN YOUR BRAND JOURNAL

It's time to do some journalling around some of these points and get it all out. Even if it feels irrelevant at the time. Put it out there on paper. You can cut it later.

Ask yourself why am I doing this?
What do I want to achieve?
Why am I different?
What do I offer that goes above what others do
in my field?

What is my business reason why?
What is driving you to make this business a
success?
How do you want to help people?

What is the transformation?

The best bit is once we've identified that drive and what we want to achieve here and the reasons for doing it, we can start to showcase it to our clients. We can start to answer their pain points from Chapter Four and show them with insane passion how we are going to help them solve them. We can show them the transformation working with us can have. It's thinking about the results they are going to get.

But why do we need to understand this? Well, because it needs to come out of our mouths every single day. Because it is our jobs as entrepreneurs to showcase to our audience that they need us, because as we know, they don't always know.

How often do you ask your clients, "How do you feel right now?" Such an easy question but when do we ever ask our customers emotionally led questions? It's always a business-focused question, right? We always try and pay it back to what we do rather than asking what they actually need. Now, I am one of those gals who get inspiration from everywhere and I remember watching New Amsterdam (an epic medical drama on

Amazon Prime that you must watch) and the very first line the new Medical Director said was, "How can I help?" So simple, but no one, no one had been asked. And we are the same. We are forever told on the internet or telling our clients on the internet what they need to do but never asking them what they want or need.

So I make a habit of asking... They don't know that those millions of tabs in their brain have a solution. I mean, who would believe that a logo or website * insert eye roll* would cause so much overwhelm and confusion? So it's my job to educate. It's my job to show them. It's my job to get them understanding that I am what they need and show them the transformation I can offer. I will close those tabs.

And all good brands do this. Take Shreddies "keeping hunger locked up 'til lunch" or Cillit Bang with their "bang and the dirt is gone." They are clever, they are catchy, but essentially it's a transformation. I mean no one wants to be dipping into the fridge for a mid-morning slice of brie, do they? We want to wait for lunch.

IN YOUR BRAND JOURNAL

So what is your transformation and how can you show that to your clients? How can we think about what we can offer them?

The I.AM.Me Brand Filter

It's not just a case of answering all of these questions and then scribbling down that full stop again in angry black marker. Now we have to put it all together. We need to find a way to communicate all of this. We need to be able to say it simply and easily without confusion. So if someone says, "What do you do?" you can come back with the most kick-ass message they've ever heard that leaves them frothing at the mouth to work with you. You may have heard this called several things: an elevator pitch, your mission statement, your brand message, but I like to call this The I.AM.ME Brand Filter. Why? Because it's exactly what it is. A statement that showcases who you are and what you do that you use as a filter from here on out that you run absolutely everything through. So we are not left at networking meetings or in online spaces going, "Well, I do this, and I do this, and it all gets pulled together a little bit like this and then I add some sprinkles and a cherry on top and... oh! Sorry, am I confusing you? You look a bit lost?" Who's been the subject of one of those? Who's been that person floundering for the words to say?

Well, I want that to never happen to you again. Introducing the I.AM.ME brand filter. It goes a little something like this.

YOU + YOUR MISSION x THEM = YOUR IMPACT.

And broken down we've got...

YOU = Who you are and what do you do.

YOUR MISSION = What results do you want to have. What are you trying to achieve here?

THEM = Who is your ideal client?

YOUR IMPACT = What changes does it make? What impact does working with you or buying from you have on their lives?

And to give you an example of how you put that all together, here is my example:

A brand expert and champion of women, empowering you to unlock your full potential by building a brand that looks, feels and sounds like you. It's time to transform your business by being true to who you are.

Or:

YOU: A brand expert and champion of women

YOUR MISSION: empowering you to unlock your full potential

THEM: by building a brand that looks, feels and sounds like you.

YOUR IMPACT: It's time to transform your business by being true to who you are.

The best bit is, if you've really journalled and worked through all of the questions in the rest of this chapter, then a lot of that will then give you the answers to the sections above... winner, winner! So no more Ronseal. Let's add a bit of Dulux sparkle into your brand statement and your clients' lives.

I don't want you sitting there after this, putting this book down and doing nothing else with this work. Because this is powerful. And I promise you there is something different about each and every one of you. Because I see you. I see your spark, I see your passion, I see your potential. Why? Because I see it in every woman who decides it's time to make a change. It's time to show the true you. I can't wait to see you.

IN YOUR BRAND JOURNAL

It's time to piece it all together. You are looking at one snappy and easy to understand sentence based on The I.AM.ME Filter.

THE I AM ME FILTER

YOU

Who you are and what you do.

+

YOUR MISSION

What results do you want to have? What are you trying to achieve here?

X

THEM

Who is your ideal client?

=

YOUR IMPACT

What changes does it make? What impact does working with you or buying from you have on thier lives?

07

THE WONDER WOMAN
JOURNEY

You are a Wonder Woman. FACT. You may not feel it yet, you may not even know it yet, but inside you right now is a super woman dying to get out. She has a calling, a mission and she is dead set in achieving it. Why else would we be doing this business, if we didn't have that entrepreneurial drive? Goals bubbling under the surface ready to be achieved? And those superpowers inside us that we can use to help others? Well, quite frankly, without those, we might as well be back in the rat race, climbing up the corporate ladder. But we are not. We wanted to give more. Be more. Achieve more. Do something for ourselves. For our customers. We wanted to offer something that our ideal customers need and it's that drive, talent, personality and energy that makes you who you are. That is your superpower. It's that fire in your belly that you feel every time you hit a hurdle, every time something doesn't go to plan, that drives you forward. That makes you one of the few people in this population who can pick themselves up, dust themselves off and learn the lesson they needed to learn. Because we've got something no one else has.

You are a Wonder Woman.

And it's all of these things that make everyone fall in love with you. It's this fire, passion and mission that make you the woman you are today. No matter who you are, no matter your shape or size, no matter what your business model is. YOU are the thing that brings the people in. You are the face of that business, the drive behind that business. And it's you and you alone who is going to get you to where you want to be.

But to get to that point, to achieve that dream scenario, we need to make sure our clients know who we are. You've heard person after person, time and time again, talk about how people buy from people. Better yet, people buy people. Yet, I can't even count the number of times I hear people saying that their business isn't where they want it to be. Or that they are putting out content on social media all day, every day and busting their balls, but the clients just ain't' coming.

YOU ARE
A WONDER
WOMAN

—

Well, let me tell you, ladies, there is only one reason for that. It's because you are not telling them your story. You are not shining a light into who you truly are. They don't know you. You are not relating to them. You are not showing them you understand how they feel. So even though you've heard time and time again that people buy from the people they love, we hide all that makes us special under a caveat of who we think we need to be. We never show the true side of who we are. And what we are constantly falling in the trap of or are at risk of putting out, is offer after offer, post after post, examples of work after examples of work and sounding more like a Selly Sally than an epic, inspirational Wonder Woman.

So I am hoping you are sitting there reading this, nodding along. I am hoping you are starting to realise that something has got to give. That all that fire in your belly needs to start coming to the surface. That you want to truly feel like Wonder Woman and you want to connect with your clients like never before. You want them to know that you've got them. Well then, ladies, it's time you start speaking to them.

It's time you start telling your story.

And before you tell me you don't have one, remember that every single woman has a powerful story. Something they've been through, something they've overcome, a special memory, you name it. Every. Single.

Woman reading this book has something inside them that can build a connection with their audience like no other person can. But the likelihood is, you've not even seen the relevance of yours, you've not even touched the surface of its huge potential. I bet some of you will even need another quick check in on Chapter Three as you've found that imposter devil again: "Who'd want to hear about me?"

Yep, I've been there. But you've got this far into this book now, that I bet you are starting to feel something inside your belly telling you, "Damn, girl, you are pretty special. There's potential here, bigger than I realised. I think it's time I start taking a bit of action on this."

I'm right, aren't I?

So where do you start?

Well, the first thing I need you to understand is that you don't need to tell all of your story. I think there is a bit of a misconception about what your brand story truly should be. A lot of the time the old wounds come out, and the storytelling starts on all the things that you think are important to you. And that's the lesson and the big tip right there. *They are important to you.* And sometimes, as harsh as this seems, what is relevant to you isn't always relevant to your clients. And when we tell too much of our story and it doesn't connect with them or they can't see the benefit of you telling it we risk putting them off. Or, and this is even worse, we end up writing a mini autobiography picking out every little step from birth to right this second and we tell it all. And then this happened, and then this happened. You've been on the receiving end of that, right? And you nod along but then the next thing comes up and the next thing and it leaves you wondering when it's going to end and why they are telling you.

Well, don't get me wrong, I am all about telling your story but it needs to be the right bits. The golden nuggets of information. The moments that resonate with your client, or that you can pay back to them in some way.

Let me give you an example... When I had Betty Lou Design, I never told the story about my Dad. There was never any mention of how little girls should be seen and not heard. Because despite its power and lessons now, for a bride to be, all excited about picking out all of her pretty details for her big day, it wasn't relevant. It sounds harsh but it didn't matter to her. She may have felt sorry for me, we may even have had a conversation about it, but deep down would she have wanted to hear it? Would she have wanted to know? Was there a payback to her in her excited, magical situation? Nope.

But what I did do was talk about the phenomenal cheerleader Betty, my Gran. I spoke about how we had her there in our own little way on our Wedding Day. I also spoke about my childhood creating art and how it was one of the only things that would keep me quiet for longer than five minutes. And I spoke about how we didn't want a traditional wedding. We wanted something that reflected us, that was unique to us with all of our own little touches, and the best bit: how we made all Rob's Northern lot travel five hours to come and be there because it was the only venue I found that I liked. All of the things that allowed them to understand why I did what I did, where my passion for what I did came from and give them a little glimpse into who I was.

So before we go on a rampage of getting that story out of you, just remember that WE get to pick the parts of our story we tell and we get to decide how much we are comfortable with telling. But we also have to remember that not all stories are negative stories. And you can still have the best stories inside you even if you haven't had a past of drama, chaos or adversity. In fact, there are seven basic plot twists in the world. Even the films you watch fit into one or more of them. And you won't be surprised that only one of them is a tragedy. So use these as a guide for when you move on to starting your story.

The seven plot twists

1. **Overcoming the monster** - Overcoming the monster is the classic hero vs villain plot. We're talking Rocky, or James Bond. It's about defeating your nemesis and emerging victorious. So what does that mean in a business sense? Well, it's all about feeling the fear and doing it anyway. For all of us, when we start off, there is something we hate to do. Something that scares us, that we avoid at all costs, and that is our monster. By identifying what that is, we can start to fight back, start to deal with it and stop it holding us back.

2. **Rags to riches** - If you want the perfect rags to riches film, think Cinderella. Going from nothing to having everything you could ever want. This is the journey we're all on. Every business starts in the same place – no clients, no orders, just the passion and hard work of the person running it – that's YOU by the way. And there's no stopping us making it to the top. The only problem is that we don't have a fairy godmother coming to give us a boost up the ladder (well, I don't, I don't know about you). We have to put in those hard yards and have our goals in our sights.

3. **The Quest** - We're all here for a reason. We all have a mission, or a big goal, something that

we want to achieve. And we're all driven by a big why. The thing that motivates us to keep going. To keep showing up day in, day out and not hiding away in a dark room. When that alarm goes off and you feel like you've had your eyes closed for thirty seconds, your big why and your quest is the thing kicks you out of bed and gets your arse in gear.

4. **Voyage and return** - Your business is a journey – I say that a lot, because it's true. It's not a one-stop shop, there's no magic solution. It takes time to lay the foundations, and it takes time to refine the rest. You always have to move forwards. Challenge yourself and break new ground, because it's only when you do that, that you can grow and scale what you do. The great thing is that every day you take a step forward, every day the voyage continues, you'll be exposed to new experiences and new problems to solve.

5. **Rebirth** - One of my favourite plots of all time. Why? Because it's the plot to one of my favourite films. And what's that, I hear you all ask? Four words. Beauty and the Beast. But what does it mean from a business sense? Well, for me, it's all about what came before all of this. Not the whole journey, but what did you learn from your life before launching your

business that makes you an expert now you've been reborn as an entrepreneur?

6. **Comedy** - Who doesn't love a comedy, eh? You know that cringeworthy moment you are laughing so hard you are a bit nervous you might wee yourself? Like Bridget Jones and her big panties and, let's face it, some unfortunate luck. Well, sometimes in life you've got to just stop and laugh. And it's the same in business. When you're being you, and I mean 100% unapologetically you, you can't take yourself too seriously.

7. **Tragedy** - Of course, tragic things happen and sometimes telling these stories can be one of the most powerful, inspiring things you can do. Because we have to remember that we never know who is listening who needs to hear what you have to say. My big tip? Only start talking about and telling these stories when you feel 100% comfortable. When you've dealt with that tragedy or are on the other side of it. When you can use it as a lesson for your clients. Just like me with my *little girls should be seen and not heard* from Chapter One. Now? It's more than just a tragic story, it's an empowerment piece that helps others to realise that we should always be using our voices.

Right, let's get back to that Wonder Woman Journey

So now we know the types of stories we can tell, I want to introduce you to a method called your No Holds Barred story. The part where you just get it all out. You may hit some hurdles, some blocks or worries if you just try and start without doing this crucial step. You'll second guess yourself. That is completely normal. So the best thing we can do is start getting it out on paper. I always tell my clients to write all their story, in a bulleted list. Think of it as your then to now journey. Start from your first significant memory and pull right through to today. Because it's only when we have it all in front of us that we can identify the parts of our story that our audience will be able to identify with it. The parts that they need to hear, even if they don't know it yet themselves.

1. **Just go for it.** No holds barred. Nothing off limits, you never know what might be relevant.
2. **No editing.** It doesn't matter how long it is, because we're only going to use certain parts of it as our journey evolves.

It's time to write your No Holds Barred bullet pointed story. Try not to overthink it. This part of the process is about getting everything out on a page.

The Story Selector

So we've got all these little gems of information; now what? It's time to get brutally honest with yourself. It might feel uncomfortable and you might find yourself continuously questioning whether you should leave it on the list. But remember that it is our minds saying it is important. We've got to get real with ourselves. What parts of this actually play into your business? What ones are going to serve or relate to those clients best? Go back to your ideal client from Chapter Four, look at who they are, what their pain points are and ask yourself some questions as you go through everything you've written down.

Have you been where your clients are now?
Did you overcome the same adversity that they face?
Did you transform your life in some way?
Are you doing this for your kids or your family?
Was there a realisation moment when you finally thought, f*ck it! I'm doing this for me?

What was the turning point that made you just go for it and launch this business?

Has something held you back and now you are stronger for it?

Or it could just as simply be something you've faced or experienced that's made you realise you'll never be the same in your business or that's spurred on your reason for doing this.

IN YOUR BRAND JOURNAL

Let's get picky! What parts of your story are relevant to your clients? As you are cutting out the parts that aren't, ask yourself the above questions. If it doesn't cut it, then it's got to go!

DISCLAIMER!

I just want to give you a little pause here. This is big bloomin' work you've just done. It's ok to put this chapter down, do something fun and come back to how we piece it all together later. Go grab a brew (or a glass of vino if you're anything like me) and a choccy biccy, lovely. You've earned it!

The Superhero Framework

This is the exciting bit. We have the nuggets and the moments and now we need to turn them into a story. We have to learn the framework that we need to tell that story to create some serious connection. Because if you think of every superhero you've ever loved, they've all had an origin story. Think about it. Wonder Woman, Superman, Captain America, YOU. They start off their lives, and then something happens. There is a plot twist. A turning point. They're almost always ordinary people and they experience something or see something that impacts their lives. Encourages them to make a change. And they have a lightbulb moment. It changes them and spurs them on to create a change in the world. And then they experience mini adventures along the way which become our follow up stories. Can you start to see how this comes together?

So what I've decided to do is break this down into an easy to use, three step framework that will help you tell your Wonder Woman journey...

1. **Your Rise** - This is just one of the nuggets you've picked out from your Story Selector. It could be what you were doing before this. Or when you first used the skills you use now. Perhaps something happened in your childhood, or in your 9-5: what was your spark? What impacted your life? This is your set the scene moment. Get people to picture being there.

2. **Your Mission** - You can't just tell your story for the sake of it. So why does it matter? What

is the benefit to your client? Why is it relevant and what makes it relatable? This is the point where you pay it back to them. When you tell them why you are telling it. Tell them how they might feel the same. Tell them how the situation changed and where you are now. It's the connector between the rise and the purpose of your story.

3. **Your Purpose** – This is the transformation that your story can offer. This is how it inspires or motivates or encourages them. It could be a change of mindset, behaviour or action. This is how it helps people. How you can say, "If I've been through this and come out the other end, then so can you," or, "Let's start working together to ensure we never look back again." It's almost like a non-salesy call to action.

IF YOU WANT SOME EXAMPLES OF HOW THIS PLAYS OUT IN REAL LIFE, I HAVE A FAB FREE GUIDE THAT YOU CAN DOWNLOAD BY SCANNING THE QR CODE BELOW.

YOUR RISE

This is just one of the nuggets you've picked out from your Story Selector. It could be what you were doing before this. Or when you first used the skills you use now. Perhaps something happened in your childhood, or in your 9-5: what was your spark? What impacted your life? This is your set the scene moment. Get people to picture being there.

YOUR MISSION

You can't just tell your story for the sake of it. So why does it matter? What is the benefit to your client? Why is it relevant and what makes it relatable? This is the point where you pay it back to them. When you tell them why you are telling it. Tell them how they might feel the same. Tell them how the situation changed and where you are now. It's the connector between the rise and the purpose of your story.

YOUR PURPOSE

This is the transformation that your story can offer. This is how it inspires or motivates or encourages them. It could be a change of mindset, behaviour or action. This is how it helps people. How you can say, "If I've been through this and come out the other end, then so can you," or, "Let's start working together to ensure we never look back again." It's almost like a non-salesy call to action.

Have a go at using this framework to craft a piece of social content about just one part of your story. One of those bullet points. Share it with a beautiful photo of yourself and see the results.

Your Future

BUT REMEMBER: There is no end to your Wonder Woman journey. Your brand is going to evolve every single day and we are going to live it every single day, so you need to continually tell different stories. Talk about something that happened last week, or last month, or even yesterday. Because each day your business grows. It evolves with you with every win, every challenge and even every failure. So write to the point where you are now, but know that it will be added to every day. Don't park this for the next five years and never look at it again. Tell stories every single day. Just wait until you get to Chapter Sixteen and we start talking about opening your eyes to inspiration everywhere. I can't wait!

08

ONE VISION.

Okay, I think I have a problem. In fact, I know I have! I remember once one of my email subscribers telling me off because every time I pinged into her inbox, I'd get another song stuck in her head. And from that day I consciously decided to do it less. But I've found myself falling back into the same habits with this book when trying to come up with cool Nicki James names for chapters. And now, while I write this chapter, I can't help but hear the dear Freddie Mercury's epic voice and if I am honest it's causing me some problems. Because all I now want to do is prance around my house and rather than type useful words in this chapter, I now want to just write the lyrics of One Vision.

But I haven't lost it, because if you think about it, Queen had some bloomin' good lyrics. And actually they are completely right about being, "One man, one goal", "one voice, one hope, one real decision," and, of course, "give me one vision". And I think it would actually be quite fun if we used this to break down this chapter. Why? Because I genuinely believe that we can't brand for where we are now. We have to brand for our future.

So let's break this down.

One (wo)man, one goal

What a line. And what a truth. The reason this is so important is that it's a massive part of what Just Brand You is all about... and you guessed it... that's YOU! There is no magic pill that is going to give you instant success here or catapult you to that next level of brand fame that you are looking for. There is no other person that can make this all happen for you. Only you can do it. Yes, I can give you all the tools, I can talk to you for days about how to make your big plans a reality, but only you can make it happen. Only you can bring yourself to the table. Only you can open up about who you truly are and what it is you want for this business. Only you can set your goals and just like in Chapter Six set your intentions for what you are trying to achieve.

I can't count how many times I've had conversations with people who are battling with what they are trying to achieve or it's not quite working for them and hearing, "Well, it's alright for you," as if it all seemed to fall into place for me. Like I had the top secret book that gave you all the tips on brand success. I didn't. I had hard work, I invested in the people that had the knowledge of things I knew I needed to get ahead and I had (or should I say have) one big goal.

TO HELP WOMEN TO UNLOCK THEIR FULL
POTENTIAL WITHOUT HAVING TO BE
SOMETHING THEY ARE NOT.

And I worked and worked until it happened. Until I could look back and say, "Hey, kid, you've done good, you're changing people's lives." A big, bold statement, I know, but one I am prepared to own because I'm achieving it. This is my one, big, goal. It gets worked on every single day.

And just like in business we have to set our goals and work out how we are going to achieve them with our brands too. We have to look deep inside of ourselves to work out what it is that we want. What does life look like for us when we embody being the face of our brands? Is it that we want to stand on stages? Is it that we want to work with influencers and celebrities? Is it to be the go-to expert in our fields? Or be featured in the best magazines? That's all part of creating your goals for your brand. For yourself. And it's time we start. Because all of this work means nothing if we don't have things we want to achieve by doing it. If we wake up every single morning, do the things and then go to sleep and rinse and repeat it the next day, it's pointless. You feel stuck on the hamster wheel of just going through the motions.

But we need to pause for a second, because I need to put a disclaimer here: it is COMPLETELY okay if your goal is personal or self-orientated. It is completely okay if the reason you are doing this is to go on fancy holidays or change your life for you and your family. But you need a destination. A place that drives you to put the hard work in. An end point that makes you do all the things you need to do to be the face of your business even when times get hard. A vision.

IN YOUR BRAND JOURNAL

So I want you to ask yourself, what is your goal? What's the dream here? What is on your bucket list of things you want to be ticking off? What does life look like when you get there? Who is that person standing there in your future self? What has she achieved? Who has she helped? Because that, my friends, is where we are heading. If you find this easier you could always do it as a visual representation. Head over to Pinterest and paint a picture of that dream life.

One real decision

We've done an awful lot of work to this point. And I am hoping that it's made you do a lot of thinking about who you are as a woman and what you can bring to the table. And we might be approaching some unfamiliar or untrodden ground. A place you haven't been before. It feels different. It feels massive. It feels like you have a lot to give and the goals you want to achieve seem like they might be unreachable. The little devils are creeping in saying *who are you to say this is your goal?* My, oh my, I get it!

Writing this book was just one of those moments for me. A moment when I realised I was about to step into a completely different level of myself to be the version of me sitting there typing this. And I have to be honest, it scared the crap out of me. I had moments where I didn't believe I could do it. And I honestly couldn't tell you how frustrated I have been with myself about why I was putting so much pressure on some words on paper. It brought on some full-on Wobbly Wendy moments, when I thought I wasn't good enough or thought I was a bad writer. Or questioned the book launch or started thinking would people think that what I was saying was any good. Would I provoke emotion or feelings within people? Am I even good at telling stories? Will I empower women to take action like I wanted this book to do so badly?

But you know what I realised? It wasn't really the writing that was causing those wobbles. Yes, it wasn't easy to get all the words out of my head and down on paper, but it was more than that. Because this book essentially is all the things I talk about nearly every single day in some shape or form. So I knew it wasn't that. So it's funny that upon writing this chapter, giving advice that I'd usually give to my clients when they are having these doubting moments, that I found my reason as to why I was feeling this way too.

It was the unfamiliarity of the person who had a published book with a big 2021 ahead of her. The person who was setting goals and finally smashing through the glass ceiling she'd made for herself. That person wasn't me, was it? And it could have been very easy to walk away. I am not going to lie, I considered it on many occasions but then I realised I had one real decision to make. Was I going to continue to shy away from the person I am destined to become and hold myself back or was I going to slowly and surely, piece by piece, brick by brick, unveil her to the world?

Was I going to stop playing with my version of "small" and finally do what I wanted to do? Was I going to turn that dial up once again as I reached that unfamiliar space but power through it to see what was on the other side? Well, I guess if you are reading this, I did it! And I hope that if people are still reading this in five years' time that I will still be doing it for whatever that might be looking like then. I knew upon writing this chapter that I was going to face that fear of the unfamiliar woman standing in front of me and I was going to jump into her with full force. So you see, I don't believe in sitting here and positioning myself on a pedestal above you just because you are reading my book. We are in this together. We are holding hands and embracing what we need to become to make this work. Because I've got a goal too and I can't achieve that if I hide away from it.

And neither can you.

We have to decide, right here, right now, together. That we are not going to stop ourselves from achieving our goals. That we are not going to stop ourselves from living within that brand we want to create for ourselves and that actually we have every possibility to be familiar with the woman we want to become. And that if we stop thinking of it as this big, huge and enormous thing and break it down into those steps I was just telling you about that actually we can achieve what we set out to do. So whatever our goal is, whatever it is we want to do, we just have one real decision to make. Are we going to achieve it?

Give me one vision

Okay, so we've set these goals, we know what we want our brand to embody, we know what we want to achieve and we know who we want to serve. Well, what now? We have to set our vision. And this is where most people fall short. Because now is the time to step outside of our safety bubble. Because I imagine most of you reading this are going to be already serving some customers in some sense. Or if you are not there just yet, it's because you feel you are not big-time enough to talk to the people you actually want to serve. So what we tend to do in these instances is to brand for where we feel we belong, or brand for the people we are currently working with. Even though deep down we want to work with a different type of person.

But talking to that person feels a bit scary, because we are not there yet, right? We don't currently attract those clients at the moment. So we'd lose custom, right? We'd lose money if that happened? And that's not an option or even possible for you?

But how do we honestly think we are going to attract the people we want to work with if we carry on branding for where we are right now? For the people we serve now. See, a good brand is going to grow with you and it needs to speak to the people we want to work with. So before we move on to becoming 'brand you' we need to make sure we are thinking of the bigger picture here. We need to think about those dream people and set our vision and goals to work with them. Because this brand needs to work for you in the long game as well as the next six months. We need to be thinking about where we want to be later down the line.

I always use the analogy of Primark (although I like to call it Primarché - sounds fancier) and Mulberry (the best brand in the entire world). Because when we think about who we want to work with, we have to think about what attracts them. So if your client is a bit more high-end, perhaps a higher earner or in a higher position, we can't be branding like Primarché even if that's where WE shop as a person now. Because we won't be speaking to them. That message and aesthetic won't appeal to them. So going forward we need to be saying to ourselves, who are these people, what do they want to see and how can I speak to who I want to serve not now but later too?

WE NEED TO
BRAND FOR
OUR FUTURE SELF.
THAT UNFAMILIAR
WOMAN. BUT
IT'S REACHABLE NOW.

———

09

NO ONE LIKES A
SELLY SALLY.

"Hi, Nicki, I'd love to be able to help you. I am a hypnotherapist and I can help you lose weight so you feel less self-conscious when you do your lives. I know it is hard when you are on the larger side."

Yep, this actually happened. And despite the title of this chapter, I am not about to talk to you about bad selling techniques. We'll leave that for another book, shall we? But this would DEFINITELY be no-no number one. I can still feel to this day my rage when this random "expert" that I don't know from Adam reached into my inbox to ask me quite frankly an insanely personal question. Not just personal but also damn right rude.

Obviously, you can imagine my response, politely explaining to her that my "larger" body actually doesn't stop me showing up on lives and if she did her research she'd find I am in fact super visible. Followed by a bit of an angry virtual finger wag that Gran would have been super proud of about how insensitive her message was. I mean, who does that? And how on earth did she think this was acceptable?

But really, I need to say thank you to this Selly Sally. Because despite her being a bit abrupt with her selling and going about things in all the wrong ways, she actually really helped me. Not in a way of looking at myself and saying, "Hey, it's okay that you are a bit round in the middle," but in a way that made me think of how many other women don't show up to their audience because they are worried about their appearance. How many other women stop themselves from doing what they want to do because their nose is too big or their face just doesn't fit live streaming. This had to change. And no, I can't make that change on my own but I can damn right start talking about it and raising awareness.

Who said to be successful or to show up online we had to be stick thin? In fact, who said we had to be any particular size? Too thin, too large, too short, too tall. Agh! But seriously... do we think legends like Ashley Graham got to where they are now worrying about a little extra weight? And then it hit me... what if this woman had said this to one of my clients who didn't have the strength to shake this off and who then went into a downward spiral of showing themselves less and less?

Next step... look all over the internet and see the stereotypical display of what the "perfect" woman looks like. No wonder we are always picking holes in ourselves. We've been conditioned to do it and still are, even to this day. Then, I stumbled across this article about Nike's new plus size gym wear "normalising obesity" and I am not going to lie, I was enraged. It contained multiple comments about how now they've brought out and showcased these plus size mannequins in their flagship stores that they are in some way saying it's okay to be overweight. So let me question for a second why an "obese" lady isn't allowed to exercise? Also, because they are overweight does it mean they've eaten one too many pork pies out the packet?

And let's say for a second that perhaps it is because they like a little more food than others - then do they not have a right to exercise and be healthy to try and change that *if* they so wish to? So of course, in true Nicki James style I was straight on social media talking to my audience about how outraged I was. It was one of those lives where I may as well have been standing on the corner in Hyde Park with my soapbox out. And it's weird because it always seems to be those types of live videos when I am so passionate about something not even directly related to brand stuff that I get the most interaction. And this piece in particular led to a great comment piece in the Metro Newspaper all about this subject which just widened my message and my voice further, allowing me to impact more people with a message, albeit not my main message but one that needed to be heard.

So I guess you are wondering how I paid this back to my clients? Why did they want to hear my little rant? Well, it actually fits perfectly into my overall brand messaging. Because I don't want women to be ashamed of who they are, or told that they should be a certain way or, in this case, look a certain way. I don't want women to feel that to be successful you can't have an extra belly roll or a wart on your face. I want women to embrace everything about themselves and bring it all to the table. Because perfection doesn't sell. It alienates. It makes you unrelatable. Besides, what even is perfection? I swear, I've only got this far because I am just a normal gal trying to help people. So you can see how my audience can get behind it even though it wasn't a direct message about being your brand.

This experience got me thinking... We can't always talk about what we do if we want to make a true connection with people as actual human beings. You know, before we even think about selling to them. Because no one likes a Selly Sally, right?

You know the ones, the people with something new out every other day of the week, trying to convince you to buy the next best thing they've thought of. It gets exhausting when you open your social media feeds to just find it FULL of sales posts. Please don't confuse this with me saying you shouldn't ask for the sale at all, because I categorically think you should, but surely not every single post? But sometimes that's what I see! We seem to live in an entrepreneurial world whereby some of the social media tactics work on the basis of *look at this beautiful picture, come book me*. There's no substance, there's no truth.

I see entrepreneur after entrepreneur get fed up that their engagement isn't growing and they throw the towel in because they are not getting the clients swarm through the door, but we are not asking people to engage with us nor are we properly communicating with them. If people buy from people, then why are we all acting like this same bozo called Sally? People want to be able to resonate with you with other things outside of what you do. I can't tell you how many times I get asked by brand designers what my secret inside trick is... well, here you go, it's here for the world to see. I just talk about things I want to talk about, things I am passionate about and things that my audience can get behind and I interweave that with my more "on brand message" posts.

So yes, key messaging is crucial. That penny-drop killer "this is what I do statement" that you weave everything through: but it isn't enough. I want to take it one step further with you.

Let me introduce you to passion messages

I want to introduce you to a concept that you may or may not have considered before. Let me introduce you to passion messages. A group of smaller messages that feed off your main message. Imagine a spider diagram for a second. Your main message sits in the middle that is the heart of everything that you do. Our filter. But coming off that are a series of your passions. And as long as in some way they can relate back to your audience and what they are thinking, feeling or passionate about too and there is a reason for you telling them about it, then it WORKS.

So maybe don't tell them about your obsession with salt & vinegar crisps and rant about your love of them for a twenty minute live stream. Well, unless you are in the health and fitness industry, that is, and your rant is coming from a place of "having a treat isn't going to kill you." Now that has legs. But think about what you are truly passionate about? It could be something in your industry, it could be something that's happened in the world, or it could be something you've witnessed or been subject to. But it's so strong and powerful that it's become something you have to talk about.

Use your ideal client as a filter

But we have to do this carefully. Because the last thing we want is our clients to stare back at us and ask, "Why are you telling me this?" It's important they get an inside glimpse into the things that make us tick but remember back to those 27 touch points we discussed when I told you about Betty Lou Design. They have to get it. So if in one of those touch points they just don't understand what you are saying, then we risk confusing them and when we confuse, we lose. So that's why it is so crucial that we've really deep dived into who it is that we are trying to serve because, just like our message that we use for everything brand you, we can also use our ideal client work as a filter to understand whether our passion message is relevant or not. Will they get it? Will this passion of yours get them feeling passionate too? How can you pay this back to them? Does it make them relate to you? Are they going to be compelled to answer you? Or are they going to think you've gone off your rocker?

IN YOUR BRAND JOURNAL

There is a chance you might need to follow a bit of the Wonder Woman structure in here. Bullet point them out and then check back with yourself using some of the questions above.

So once you've identified the passion messages, you need to find your own unique way to put them out into the world, a way to showcase your opinions and make them part of your content as part of your strategy to build that all important know, like and trust factor with your audience. That could be a post, a live, an email or some PR just like mine, but the important thing is getting it out there in your own way. And telling it with courage and conviction. Owning it. But I'm not going to tell you how to do all of that just yet, there are a few other things we need to cover first. One step at a time, my lovely, one step at a time.

Here seems like a good point to hit pause and do a bit of reflection. We've just covered a lot of ground. I've just walked you through the entire first step of Just Brand You. And now I would hope you are starting to understand how important it is to put you into your brand. Because creating a brand can't just be you hiding in the shadows. We need to work out our way to stand out in the sea of sameness. To no longer fear our competition, because our only worry will be how far we are willing to go to achieve the success we desire. Whatever that looks like.

Define Brand You came about because as women we don't spend enough time showcasing our hidden magic and using everything we have inside us to get into that untouchable lane.

And there is a reason why this section takes up over half of the chapters in the book. It's because it's the most important and without spending the time working this through there is no point moving on to Becoming Brand You. We are not creating purely logos and websites here, ladies. We are creating the next level of you. Step into it now, own it and let's start unleashing that power. You've got a mission... let's go accomplish it.

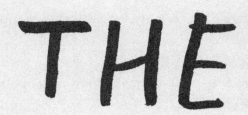

THE

I wanted to be able to provide you with a little ticklist at the end of each section of the things covered and what you need to be working on as part of Define Brand You. Remember, it's not a race to the finish line. I'd rather you take the time and do these things well, than rush them and still be left confused.

IDEAL CLIENT

1. Identifying your ideal client as a best friend - Remember we are using this for the very next chapter. What appeals to them? What is their life like? Who are they? Remember you can have more than one.
2. Identifying your ideal client's pain points - This is one of the most crucial steps of understanding your ideal client because this is how we speak to them. Why do they need you?
3. What are your ideal client's goals? - We need to be able to work out the dream scenario they want to be in, so we can help them to get there.

BRAND VALUES

1. Identify your brand values and work out what is non-negotiable for you. Your ideal client will resonate with them and also you will find it easier for business purposes, collaborations or even people you learn from going forward.

RECAP

MESSAGING

1. Why are we really doing this? What are we trying to accomplish here? How are we going to serve our clients in a way no one else can?

2. Use The I.AM.ME. Brand Filter to streamline all of your work into one easy to remember, repeatable sentence. Don't overcomplicate it here.

YOUR WONDER WOMAN STORY

1. The No Holds Barred Story - Get all of your bullet points out on paper. Everything. Don't hold back.

2. The Story Selector - Get that highlighter out and work out the ones that are relevant to what you do. Remember, there might be parts that aren't right for your main story but could be really good for social media content.

3. Write your Wonder Woman Journey - It's time to write your bio, or your about page, if you wish. What is your story? How did you get here? From then to now…

PASSION MESSAGES

1. This chapter. You need at least five passion messages that you can interweave into your content. You've got this.

NOW...

LET'S START BECOMING THIS BRAND,

SHALL WE?

———

BECOME BRAND YOU →

BECOME

BRAND

YOU

10

BECOMING
THE BRAND

Eek! We are at the start of Become Brand You. It's an exciting section of the journey, ladies, as we can start to see it all come to life. Now, within these next few chapters I want to talk to you about how you can bring everything we've just learnt together, with passion and personality. I am not necessarily going to show you how to create your own logos, or how to code your shiny new website... this book would become a range of encyclopedias if I did that and really, really boring ones too (sorry coders but it's true)! But I am going to tell you some of the things you need to be considering to ensure you stand out in a crowded market. I am going to be showing you where to source inspiration. NOTE: it is NOT from your competitors. I will show you how you bring more of you out in everything that you do, but most importantly I hope that you will be able to go away with a better understanding of what a brand truly is and know how to do it the right way.

I feel like "personal brand" has become such a buzz-word recently. It's always been there but it feels like more people are catching on to its potential now as small business owners. And you can start to see the cogs ticking in people's brains when they realise they can't just hide behind logos and fancy graphics anymore. I remember when I first started out in my industry I was one of those designers creating logos and logos alone and although they were fab there was no real essence of the woman behind them. They may have looked nice, but they didn't really say anything. See! Told you we don't always get everything right. And it's only been on my own journey with my own battles to get noticed and be seen that I've learnt all the other things that need to be included to create a true stand out brand. Because you can have the prettiest or coolest branded assets in the world but if it doesn't look, feel and sound like you, then you may as well give up now, lady. You'll continue fighting like Rocky Balboa against your competitors and will forever feel deflated about why the clients aren't queuing up at the door.

So buckle in, ladies, it's going to be a fun ride.

When the world zigs, zag!

I want to start by introducing you to one of my favourite lines from brand advertising. I absolutely adore it. I remember when my husband first told me about the iconic Levi Jeans advert (he's an advertising bod so our conversations go to ads quite often) with the one black sheep in a field of white sheep being super defiant and looking the other way. I guess this probably sums up my entire brand. I always get itchy feet the second I think I might be looking a little bit too much like someone else. But I haven't always been that way. Back in the days of comparing myself to others, I feared if I created something that was too bold or too stand out that I'd put people off. I mean not everyone loves black, white and teal. I even had someone once say that the teal reminded them of toilet bleach *and delete*.

When I first started my brand business, formerly named Branding by Nicki (a complete and utter mishap described more in Chapter Thirteen), I played it so safe. So neutral. Jeez, it didn't even look like me. As I am sure you have guessed by now I am far from neutral in character. But I thought that it's what we should do as brand experts. Be neutral. Not have anything too jazzy, nothing too out there, nothing too bold. I mean that is what everyone else was doing in my industry so that must be the done thing, right? Well, the three people I spent my days comparing myself to were anyway. So you know what I went for? The stereotypical. The obvious. Blush pink, charcoal and white! With scripted pretty fonts (trendy at the time) and beautiful clean lines.

Now don't get me wrong, I am not saying there is anything wrong with that IF it suits who you are but do I look like a blush pink gal? Seriously, go check out my Instagram @justbrandyou and tell me if I scream PINK! Hell, I've never even owned a blush pink or even a pink anything. Even as a kid I used to be infuriated if Mum bought me anything pink for Christmas... and it would work its way to the bottom of the wardrobe, never to see the light of day. I promise I wasn't an ungrateful spoiled little brat, even though that sounded like it! I just knew what I liked.

But I think I've hit the nail on the head here. I spent so much time looking at everyone else, fitting into an industry standard box, that I'd lost who I was. And I see it time and time again. Business owners from the same industry all having the same logos, the same curated social media feed and following all the same patterns. And I can't help but question it... Because imagine for a second you are your ideal client and you head on to Instagram and you start scrolling through on a hashtag for florists for your wedding day, let's say. And every man and his dog posts the same photos, of the same types of flowers, with the same colours, and the same boring old "here's a bouquet of flowers" wording and what are you left with? CONFUSION, PEOPLE! How are they supposed to pick someone if they all look the same? But if Pippa comes along with something a bit different, if Pippa comes along and stands out and breaks the mould... well, you'll be damn sure I am booking Pippa. Because Pippa has caught my eye. Pippa has stood out. Pippa stopped me scrolling. Pippa is my kind of gal!

Which leads me on nicely to probably one of the biggest points I will make in this entire chapter. When looking for your brand inspiration, stop looking at your competition and thinking that you need to do what they are doing to get ahead. To get it right. What works for them may not work for you, no matter how successful they seem! We can't all have the same personality, the same style, the same likes and dislikes so why do we try to create carbon copies of something that we think works? Because they ain't you, lovely. And we don't want them to be.

Now, don't get me wrong: no ideas are new ideas. I am not asking you to come up with something revolutionary and never seen before here. I haven't created a completely new artistic style doing what I do (I am no Andy Warhol) and it does make me chuckle when people think they have and suddenly they've created something untouchable. There's no new news, people! But what we can bring to the table that no one else can is our personality.

One of my good friends and social media whizz kids, Sam Bearfoot, shows this perfectly. She posts what she wants, when she wants and it showcases her slightly mad, very bold and pretty badass personality. She isn't for everyone and she is completely happy with that. I mean, jeez, she's even created the zero f*cks squad, a Facebook group for her raving cheerleaders and writes about cockblocking in her sales pages - don't even ask! And the best bit is that her clients tell her that they've signed up for just this reason. She wasn't always this way, but when she truly stepped inside her differentiation and embraced that difference online she had achievements many of us would envy and growth on social media platforms that you'd never believe. Genius.

So my biggest lesson when we are talking about how your brand needs to look, feel and sound like you and where to get inspiration for the aesthetics and language of your brand is to embrace that epic personality of yours and to showcase who you are. It's about what you like and what you are attracted to and the likelihood is, your clients will like it too. So whatever you do with this book take this point with you... Stop trying to fit in to everyone else's version of what you should be. You will get a million times further if you stop trying to fit into your industry box and just be you.

So where do we look for inspiration?

Well, it's simple really. Outside of the industry that you are in. So florists look at the fashion industry perhaps, wellness experts look at the coaching industry and so on. But also branch out further than this and look at magazines, brands your ideal client likes, keep your eyes open even when you are looking at packaging in the supermarket. There is inspiration everywhere. You just have to open your eyes to it. It's about digging into who you are and who they are. What does your house look like? What colours do you find yourself wearing all the time? What colours suit you? Then when you've thought about this you want to break your inspiration down in to the following categories:

Brand inspiration - Your logos and visuals.

Web inspiration - For ideas for your website and lots of it. You want to pull different parts of websites, or there could be key elements you like of a specific website.

Colours - You are probably looking at maximum 5-6 colours but with 2-3 key colours.

Patterns, Textures and Illustrations - Some brands include these if it is right for them. It's a great way to differentiate your style. Maybe a nice textured paper? Or a bold print?

Fonts - What fonts are you attracted to? Are you looking for a romantic handwritten font that gives a softer look or are you looking for a super modern and bold font? Fonts help to give huge meaning within your brand. They have very different feels. Have a look at some brands that resonate. What style of font are they using?

Your vision filter

So you've got all of this inspiration (and whilst we are on that subject I need to say that you are aiming for hundreds of bits and not just five) but what do we do with it? Well, we refine it, of course. We question piece by piece whether it sits together aesthetically, we question whether we can live with it, whether it speaks to us, would we see it in our house, on our bodies as an item of clothing. Does it compliment us? Is it conveying the right vision? And we go through a process of refine, refine, repeat. Until we have a final selection that we can pull together into a mood board: one final representation about where we are heading with our vision.

Now, I know to some of you, you may be thinking, hold on, why do I need a load of images on a page to have a vision for my brand? But it's so that going forward you have a springboard, a vision filter that you can use for your brand photography, your assets, your social media feed, well, basically anything you put out there going forward. Just like with your brand message you can check in with it to make sure that things you are creating still feel like that overarching brand look you are looking for. Because there is nothing worse than your brand feeling a little bit like a higgledy-piggledy mess. How will people recognise you then? Not to mention it's the first time you see everything come to life, which is insanely exciting!

This feels like a really good point to introduce you to Emily from Emily Bridal as I want you to know how this plays out in real life. She won't mind me saying this but she was probably one of my most challenging clients to date. And I put that down to her classic overthinking behaviour. But don't get me wrong here, this isn't negative overthinking. Every single decision we made for her brand had to be analysed and questioned against who her ideal client was. It was genius.

I remember her coming to me with a list of "requirements" for her website and thinking that it wouldn't be possible but knowing if she was going to take the plunge then it had to be this way. I think I might have dazzled her slightly. She'd never let go of the reins before. It was her baby and here I was saying, "We could do it." The sky was the limit and so was Em's to-do list. And to say it wasn't easy was an understatement. It had to reflect their personality, it had to answer all of their clients' needs, it needed to give them a real idea of what it was like to be inside the shop and it needed to let them feel like they had a safe space with real people to buy their wedding dress from. And on top of that it had to have more bells and whistles and jazzy bits than you could shake a stick at. So not much of an ask then?

But Emily knew that she needed to stay one step ahead of the curve. Emily knew she was in a competitive market and Emily knew most importantly what was going to attract her ideal client to the door. It wasn't just something you could find on Pinterest. It couldn't be a carbon copy of what she'd seen other bridal brands do before. It HAD to be different. And inspiration truly did come from everywhere. We were scouring different websites for transitions we liked, scouring others for aesthetic inspiration, plus all the random ideas coming out of our heads. Because Emily Bridal couldn't be the same. It couldn't be normal. Emily Bridal needed to be more. Was more.

Well, it ended up more and then some. Emily's website became one of my projects I am most proud of. It became a huge cog to her business, especially during the tough lockdown times. But it wasn't because it was fancy. It wasn't the bells and whistles that did this. It's because it was so in tune with her ideal client and who they were as a business that it spoke to them and only them. It did the job. It converted them. And that is the power of looking outside of your industry. For creating something stand-out. For creating something so you and so them that they are prepared to travel to see you.

You see, it's not just coaching industries that have to consider putting themselves and their clients into their brand. This works for product-based and service-based businesses alike. Emily and her team of batshit crazy girls are front and centre and everything screams, *Come see us. Yes, you! We are talking to you and we've got what you need.*

So just like Emily, I want your brand to stand out for all of the right reasons. I want people to instantly recognise a post from you. I want them to read the copy on your website and feel like they can hear you say it and I want it to scream and shout your personality. I want you to become a client magnet by being true to who you are. Let me show you how you get started with building brand you.

11

IT NEEDS TO LOOK
AND FEEL LIKE YOU

There is only one you and that is your superpower. People are going to fall in love with who you are as a person. And as much as I say that your brand isn't just your logos, visuals and assets and I bang on about this a lot, I still think they have huge importance. But only after we've worked out all that makes us tick. All of our powers from inside us. You see, to build brand visuals that create that emotional connection with your clients there are lots of things to consider. Lots of elements that differentiate just a logo to an entire visual brand suite. To get it right it needs to look, feel and sound like you and in this chapter I want to talk about the "looks" and "feels" part.

Now, there is a lot to get through so I am going to break it down into individual points. I hope that by the end of this chapter you'll either be able to go away and work on the bits you need to within your visuals or brief someone epic and go to them with courage and conviction in what you are looking for.

Building a brand is like falling in love

I remember when I first heard this quote on Aaron Pierson's podcast *Branding like a Boss* and it just clicked. It summed up everything that I wanted to be able to say to my audience in such a clever way. Because building a brand with you at its heart involves creating an emotional connection with your audience. They need to feel like they know who you are, like they can feel your personality and they can see every single part of it in everything you put out there.

See, your brand, just like dating, has a series of touch points and let's face it no one goes on one date, falls in love instantly and gets married and has babies, do they? Nope! It takes a series of dates, the feelings grow, you keep seeing them and one day, BAM! The butterflies come and you realise for the first time that this might be the real deal. So your brand needs to be the same. You almost need your brand to feel like your dating profile. You need to stop having an online presence that looks how you think it should look and start making it look like who you are. Because your dating profile is the thing that is going to speak for you when you aren't in the room with someone, your visuals, assets and things you put out there into the big online world need to be easily recognizable by your admirers. So they know when your posts are coming. They need to be able to understand who you are and what you are like just by looking at your online presence.

So how do we do this?

Say Cheese

Let's start with the easy part, brand photography. Gone are the days when a cheeky iPhone shot is going to cut it. Or the pro-shot from your wedding day. Now every entrepreneur worth their salt has a suite of brand images that they splash all over their social media feeds showing their beautiful glowing faces to the world. But I've got a problem. A really big, ranty problem. THEY ALL LOOK THE SAME! Please tell me why, oh why, every woman decides that it's time for their brand shoot, put on their best blazer and sit in a lush looking cafe, laptop on the table, with their massive cup of coffee (that they don't even drink or even worse they don't even like) and beam lovingly into the foamy cup. And yet again, another stereotypical shot pops up on my Insta feed as I am scrolling through. Are we playing an online game of snap that I don't know about?

STOP BEAMING INTO THE FOAMY CUP!

Now, I don't mean to be mean and I am aware I sound a bit like a knob in writing this and I don't really have this huge problem with the coffee cup shot. As long as it is actually true to who you are and what you do. So ask yourself, do you actually go and sit in a coffee shop and work? If so, fine. I will let you off. But I feel it's become the go-to entrepreneurial pose. That and the fake posed desk shots of you tippity-tapping away with everything exactly in the right place. It's just not real life is it? And I bet it isn't a reflection of the person's true personality.

Yet we all do it. Christ, I even did it. I was one of those people absolutely petrified of the camera. I put so much pressure on myself. Ordering 50,000 outfits from ASOS, overthinking where we were going to do it, battling my hatred of how I looked, and I too went down the stereotypical route. Heading on to Pinterest to find inspiration on "female brand photography," looking at what others were doing and sending back everything apart from the obvious power blazer. I was a bloomin' stationer at the time, spending most of my nights scrubbing paint off of my hands after creating my next piece of artwork. Yet here I was meeting my photographer, with my curled hair, make up done, power blazer on and high heels. I did wear ripped jeans, though, which I found myself editing out at every opportunity just in case it put people off. And you know what? On that shoot I felt awkward. Uncomfortable. I didn't feel like me and it showed. All over the photos. I've even got a *bloomin' coffee cup shot* and the *stare up to the ceiling lovingly looking at the spider in the corner shot.* Why do we do it? Why do we think by conforming to what the perfect brand photo is that we are by some miracle going to attract our customers? It led me to a point of dreading having my photo taken and it should be a really fun experience.

I ended up doing a flatlay shoot for my next shoot with the photographer because I just felt so awkward behind the lens. When I look back now, I can see that the reason I hated having my photo taken so much was because I was trying to squash every single part of my personality. I was trying to be something I was not. I was conforming. And in turn, yes, I may have had some beautiful photos, but they didn't do me any service. Those of you that are this far into the book by now probably have gone to follow me on social media (I hope). And if you have, and you've seen me speaking on a Facebook Live, you have probably realised that I've got a bit of a character. I am bubbly, fun, and a bit excitable at times. And don't even think about me trying to be serious as I've probably got the worst resting bitch face you've ever seen. I will stare straight down that lens and look like you've just cancelled Christmas. Seriously.

We have to show our personality

I had my biggest lightbulb moment when I realised I could do it my way. When I realised I didn't need to do what other people were doing and that I could just be me. My following shoot, I was pulling funny faces, sticking my tongue out and belly laughing left, right and centre. And I actually enjoyed myself. It took all of the fear away because I was just being me. Having fun. And the best thing was that when I showed these photos online they had the best response. One person who bought my 100% Brand You Group Program even went as far to say that she saw me online through a friend of a friend and knew she had to work with me just because of my brand photos. They showed my personality. They showed the real me. And that got people's attention.

So I want you to ask yourself, whether you are planning a shoot or whether you have brand photos currently, is it you? Are they in a location you'd actually be seen in? Are you wearing clothes that don't just flatter your body but also look like something you'd actually wear. And how could you bring more of your personality to the table.

I want to tell you about one of my clients who has done this and done it really well as a source of inspiration for you.

I want to introduce you to my client Emma from Fondant Cake Design. Emma joined my group program at a point where her business needed to change. Not because it wasn't successful, in fact the complete opposite. She was inundated with clients but it needed to change in order to suit her lifestyle. Where she could work with the right clients who wanted what she truly wanted to offer. You see, when you brand your business it isn't just because it isn't working. It could be for many reasons such as change of direction, development, levelling up, you name it.

Emma was one of those phenomenal action takers. She understood what it was to be different but also was one of those lucky ones who got a lot of custom perhaps without ever embracing her face in her business. She realised that to step out from celebration cakes and solely position herself into the wedding industry that her face was going to have to become a little more present. One of the things that I get people to do when thinking about what their brand photography is going to look like is to go away and get inspiration. To think outside the box and think of what you want to portray. In such a crowded market, it was obvious to Emma that she needed to embrace her infectious, fun personality. She is quite tongue in cheek, she doesn't take herself too seriously and she has some of the best relationships with her clients. She needed people to see that.

What Emma came back with was just phenomenal. It wasn't just a lady standing in her kitchen, mixing cake mixture or creating sugar flowers. She went into the woods, with her epic cakes and a bag of flour and she threw it all over herself. Actual cake in the face! And it was amazing. Soon after working together, Emma did a wedding show where, for the first time, she showcased her photographs along with her beautiful cakes. A real stand-out presence that grabbed people's attention and started a connection. It wasn't just the obvious "seen it all before" stand. And that's it really, isn't it? It's about standing out and not blending in. It's about finding your way to make people step into your world and start that conversation with you.

Emma Somers, Fondant Cake Design

Who's the right person for the job?

Just like when you are finding the right brand designer, you have to find the right brand photographer too. They need to have the right edge. You don't want light and fancy if you are a cool, edgy brand but also you want to ensure that they are asking you the right questions in order to understand all about you. Do they want to know all about your brand or are they just trying to take your picture? Go armed with strong ideas, a vision for how you want it to look and an energy you want it to have. Have all of your Define

Brand You work ready to share with them. They want to know all about you. But most importantly make sure it's someone you feel comfortable with. That your personalities match. Because they might be the best photographer but they are going to get the most out of you if you like what they are about.

The dreaded edit

Have you ever found yourself picking holes in every single little thing about yourself? A good friend of mine the other day spoke about how she exercises all the time and is super healthy but still finds things about herself she doesn't like. I could have spat my tea out because I look at her and think she is perfect. But this is just what we do as women. We see all the things in ourselves that no one else sees. I don't know about you but I am a picker. I look at every single photo of myself and analyse every part of it. My nose looks too big, my arms are too fat, my chubby chops are showing (a Nicki way of explaining that horrid bulge you get under your neck when you smile and move your face back - you know the one). But I know I am not the only one who does it. I think we all do. But what we have to remember is that your clients probably aren't picking those things up. They see the infectious smile, the glint in the eye, the spark that you bring and they will connect with you on it.

Also, a huge thing we need to remember here is how your audience is looking for a real person. Not Power Suit Pauline. Someone they can relate to, someone who isn't perfect. A real human being. So be more you, embrace your face and show people your true version of yourself.

The logo game

I want you to picture for a second a 330ml Coca Cola can. The bright postbox red, the white scripted logo, the sexy gardener with his top off. Oh no, wait! That's Diet Coke. But all jokes aside, I want you to picture it. Now imagine that rather than Coca Cola, it said Nicki. Would you still look at the can and think it's Coca Cola? Of course you would! I mean we all did when they brought out their personalised cans in 2014. Because Coca Cola aren't just known for their iconic logo. What about Santa Claus? Yep, Coca Cola created the visual of what Santa looked like when they commissioned illustrator Haddon Sundblom to put a face to the legend in 1931. And now we all get excited about the Coca Cola Christmas van. They created that part of Christmas and we mark it as an "okay it's officially Christmas" sign once we see the ad on TV.

Okay, okay, I digress, but my point is Coca Cola isn't just recognised for one thing. We need to be able to strip out that one individual part of your brand identity and it still feel like it's yours. So one logo and one logo alone, isn't all that makes that happen. It's the fonts you use, the colours you choose, the patterns you play with and the assets you create that get you noticed and remembered as a brand and not just this one element.

So what do you need and what should you avoid at all costs?

I'm going to break down some of the things you need to consider including and most definitely EXCLUDING within your brand in order to end up with something recognisable. To get noticed. To get remembered. To create something iconic and to truly start being a little more you and a lot less them.

You need a three piece suite of logos

Your brand is not hugely dissimilar from a comfy couch. A good couch, as we know, needs more than one cushion to make it work. And your brand suite is completely the same. And typically, when I was thinking about how I could explain this I realised that I could break it down into three parts. Winner, Winner! Enter my three piece suite. Now I can't count the number of enquiries I've had with, "Can you design me a logo?" Well, no! No, I can't. Because I'd be doing you a disservice. Or even, "Do I need a logo?" Of course you do. That's your mark, your stamp, your tag to put on everything that is yours so that people identify you. It grabs attention, makes a strong first impression and is quite honestly expected from your audience.

It becomes the foundation of your brand identity. But a logo alone isn't enough. Let me tell you the three things that you need and why.

1. **A primary logo** - So we all know what this one is. It's your main logo and the most "complete" logo of all of your suite. Usually this will include your business name and perhaps a tagline. Generally, this is the one you are going to use on your website headers or any printed materials you use.

2. **An alternative logo** - Essentially it is what it says on the tin. It's an alternative to your main logo. So if your logo is big and long and you are looking for a more compact or more square logo to fit into different spaces this is where this comes in.

3. **A submark (or monogram)** - This is going to be your simplified mark that works as a watermark on images or something that you use on social media posts or in your footer. It could be part of your logo's illustration (just like the Nike Swoosh) or your initials.

Every logo deserves to bloom

Something I notice a lot with logos is that there isn't a huge amount of differentiation from the initial font to the finished product. Now as much as I love typography and there are some absolutely stunning fonts out there, we can't own fonts and only have them for our brands. We can't suddenly stop everyone else from using that font. So we need to be able to add flourishes to our brand that make it our own. It might be editing the font as an example, taking out the middle of an A or adding additional elements like illustrations or a pattern to make it unique to you. Because you need this brand identity to not be easily repeatable. You need it to feel iconic and noticeable. You need it to feel yours. There need to be elements that make it a logo and not just a typed out font.

Simple is sometimes the only option

When thinking about your visual brand identity we have to consider how it's going to look at various sizes. One of the biggest mistakes I see businesses make is they end up with a logo so busy with bells and whistles that it starts to look cluttered, unidentifiable and illegible. We need to consider where this is going to be used, how it is going to be seen and on what devices. A logo shouldn't have all of the elements of your brand crammed into it. You just need to KISS it - Keep It Simple, Stupid. Not that I'm calling you stupid there, it's just a phrase I have in the back of my mind whenever I'm designing. It can be so easy to overthink or over complicate it, but often, when it comes to logos, simpler is better.

We have minimal time to gain attraction from people when they see our logo, so the last thing we want them to be doing is trying to decipher what it is, or what it says. We want them to recognise it, to know it's us and to engage with what we have to say because they recognise us. Whether that's saving our post, liking our post, commenting on something, or simply registering us in their brain for the perfect moment when they need what we can offer.

I want to paint a rainbow

Have you ever seen one of those brands that look like a rainbow has puked up on it? Well, when we talk about emotional connections we need to consider the thing people notice first. Colour. So as a brand we need to ensure that, "Oh, my goodness" isn't the first thought that comes to mind.

Subconsciously, as human beings we notice the colour something is before we even see what it is we are looking at. Think of it a little like a traffic light. Red we know is danger, amber is to be ready and green is go, go, go. So it's obvious that this is where most people start with brand building. The colours they are going to use. It's called colour psychology and my Christ it's a beast to explain. But we can't get hung up on the science and stop ourselves from ever coming up with a brand colour palette. We need to first start by picking things that we like, colours we are attracted to, that we live with and that we surround ourselves with if we are going to build a brand that looks and feels like us. AND then, and only then, can we start to do our research into what these colours mean. And when doing that you can think of how you want your brand to feel from some of our Define Brand You work and select around two to three main colours, used within your main identity, and a maximum of three secondary colours that might be used within your other graphics and visuals.

But here is the trick with colour psychology and why I don't want you to get too hung up on it. The truth is there can't actually be a set rule. Having a colour palette that sits bang on with colour psychology "rules" is an impossible task. Yes, colour experts will have analysed people's responses to certain shades, hues and tones of colour for many years and yes, there is some definite science around how it works, but actually, people's reactions and emotions to colour works on a person by person basis. It works on how our brains see that colour individually and our past association with colour. Think of it like one of those ink blot tasks you did as a kid and they ask you to say what you see in it and everyone sees something different. It's the same with how people feel about colour.

Yet people spend hours and hours getting stressed out and bogged down in whether they use blue in their brand colour palette because it gives a cool, serene feel to it in one hue but also could be seen as trustworthy and intelligent when it's a richer, deeper shade. For instance, many well-known brands use red. It can give a feeling of excitement and power and I bloomin' love my post box red jumpsuit: it gives me that exact feeling, but let's face it, red also makes you think of blood and danger.

So what's the solution? I'd rather you pick colours that feel like you and embody who you are, than fall down the colour rabbit hole and end up with something that you'd never be seen dead in but ticks all the boxes on a scientific scale. People buy from people, ladies, and that person is you.

Be a trendsetter and not a trend follower

Do you remember when Pantone's colour of the year came out in 2018 and it was ultraviolet? I think it was the first year I've ever thought they'd lost the plot. And if you didn't hear about it, google it and seriously tell me how it became colour of the year. THE YEAR!

At the time I was working at the food magazine, Olive, and I remember the team trying so hard to make something work on the front cover in order to follow the design "trend". But what food do you know that sits lovingly with purple apart from a Dairy Milk bar? And this happened year after year in all of my corporate life. Pantone would announce their colour and we'd all scramble around to make it work, even if it meant reshooting or delaying the print deadline ahead of their big announcement.

It's not just the editorial world, it's the same for hair... Remember when having silver hair was a huge thing and suddenly every man and his dog wanted it? I believe my Mum even decided there and then to go grey despite years of dying her hair. We seem to live in a world of trend followers in order to fit in and we seem to think by being trendy that we will capture more attention. But the people who really make it set the trends and don't just follow them. They are not following the latest thing in fashion or the next glossy page in Elle Decoration. Or the latest style that everyone else is doing. So I just wanted to touch upon being really careful when creating your visuals to not make your decision based on what is the in thing at the time. Because just as quickly as trends come in, they can leave.

And your brand deserves a much longer shelf life.

So go out there, be bold, find your style, grab that inspiration from industries outside of your own. But most importantly, remember this is a visual representation of you. No one else.

12

IT NEEDS TO
SOUND LIKE YOU

Tonight Matthew, I'm going to be...

There should only be one answer to this and if the answer was anyone other than your own name then go back to Chapters Two, Three and Six and remember how amazing you are. See, I want to take this right back to some of the things we fall into the trap of when we are starting out in this online space. Because contrary to popular belief, we are not on an episode of Stars in their Eyes and as much as I love the idea of dressing up as Tina Turner and shimmying in my gold sequin dress to Proud Mary, I have to admit to myself right now that I could never pull that off. Just as I could never pull off sounding like anyone else but myself in this online space, unless I just outright copy them, but no one likes a copycat. And no one really deep down wants to be one either. But for some reason when we come into this online space we get so influenced by everyone around us that we get engulfed into the sea of sameness. Where everyone who does what we do ends up sounding the same.

And when we fall into the trap of not knowing what to say, we subconsciously fall back onto things we've heard. The other thing that obviously happens here, is that we fear saying what we truly want to say, so we say nothing at all. And where does that leave us? Frustrated, sad and not moving forward.

But there is another way. You could stop putting pressure on yourself every time you sit down to write a social media post or you stare at that blank white page of copy and you could realise that all you need to do is sound like yourself to become a client magnet. Use your little analogies, your weird and wonderful ways of explaining things and speak from the heart and not from the "I should be saying this" place.

It's a known fact by many marketers that people are first influenced by image. That is what makes them stop the scroll. The second thing they look at is the top line. That's the hook and makes them want to read on. And finally, the rest of your post/piece of copy where you are talking to them in more detail is where you hook them in. You take them on an emotional journey that gives them that famous "me too" moment. You see, copy has that power. A picture can paint a thousand words but some cracking copy can tug on their heartstrings and get them engrossed into your world.

Copy can be the difference between someone buying from you or not buying from you and it's our jobs as entrepreneurs to have relatable moments with our audience, to show them that we understand and to show them who we are as normal human beings by adding all our little quirks into it. But most importantly, copy is our chance to show our audience what we have to offer. Why we should be the ones serving them.

And if we think about all of the touch points* that our clients need to see us on, apart from live videos copy is a part of every single thing that we put out there on a daily basis. It sits on our websites, our sales pages, our social media posts, our emails, you name it. But yet when most people sit down and write copy they go monotone, boring, stereotypical or they shy away from it altogether. But clever copy is going to be absolutely game changing for your brand and it doesn't have to be as hard as we make it. Yes, I know we are not all born writers but I want you to remember something really simple here. It just needs to sound like you.

*A touchpoint is every single time your client sees you. Remember, building a brand is like falling in love.

If you wouldn't say it, don't type it.

Imagine for a second you are sitting in a pub with your mates. Laughing. Joking. Talking with confidence and ease. It's really rare in those instances we stop ourselves from saying what we truly want to say. It's really rare in those instances that we speak to them as our "higher selves." We talk to them like human beings, like friends. And that is the exact same way you should talk to your clients. Because, shocker... they are real individuals too and they are craving someone real, honest and awesome like you to come in, scrap the industry jargon and talk to them like normal people. So if it wouldn't come out of your mouth in normal conversation, then it shouldn't be typed on a page. A great tip for this is to read it back out loud. If you stumble around when you say it, then it's because it isn't coming naturally to you. It's about remembering who you are. If you are humorous, use humour. If you swear, then throw in an F* bomb here and there. And if, just like my beautiful client Emma Wakefield, you like all things spiritual and woo then share that with the world. We don't need to hide these parts of us. These people want to hear from the real you.

But I get it, okay? When you are staring at a blank page and you have a thousand word sales page in front of you, it can be very difficult to think at that moment, "What do I need to say?" So a big tip here is to use something like Otter.ai. It's a fab website where you can talk straight into the app and it translates it for you. Winner, winner! Just maybe don't take it to the pub? No one wants to relive the drunken transcript.

What you are aiming for with good copy is that your reader takes it all in and by the time they get to the end of the post or page, they feel like they know who you are. They feel like they can hear you saying it. They feel a connection to what you are saying. They now know you are the gal for them. And sometimes, when you have three people you are considering for the job, it comes down to that all important personal connection that seals the deal. So no more telephone voice. No more what you think you should say. It's what you want to say, how you'd naturally say it and stop fretting about it not being polished or perfect. It's just you.

KISS it.

It's safe to say that no one likes a waffle. Well, unless it's a potato one and then it's fair game. But have you ever read a page on someone's website and it doesn't seem to go anywhere? It feels a little like it's being padded out to make it go further? It's really common to fall into a waffle trap where you go off on a tangent and never bring it back. Now, don't get me wrong, I like a bit of fluff and an analogy as much as the next person, but probably my biggest tip for you about copy is just the same as your visuals: it's sometimes easier to keep it simple! We always try and over explain or over complicate everything we write. Perhaps it's fear of not sealing the deal or sounding like we know what we are talking about? Or perhaps it's too much use of flowery language or industry jargon that we throw into the mix to make ourselves sound more knowledgeable? But the best way to use your words to make people get it is to cut out all of the unnecessary rubbish and keep it as short and sweet as possible.

IF SOMETHING CAN BE SAID IN ONE SENTENCE. DON'T SAY IT IN THREE.

Forget everything you've ever learnt

You are no longer at school. There is no one here with a red pen. I write this knowing full well that my right-hand woman is proofreading this for me, who used to be a deputy head teacher, but apart from her, NO ONE is judging you on what you learnt at GCSE or A-Level. And it's about time we forgot a lot of the English Language protocol we had drilled into us as children. You see, it's like driving a car. You do everything perfectly when you are in your lessons and to pass your test, things like hands at ten and two, but then when it comes to driving in the real world those hands might slip a bit to some different times of the day. It's the same with language. We don't need to speak like we've swallowed a dictionary or chewed up our English teacher. So let me break this down into some key things I want you to banish from your brain right now and you can start implementing.

Short sentences add punch

Gone are the days where every sentence needs to have a connecting word in it. And, but, because. In fact, shorter punchier sentences with as few as two or words in them when interspersed can have more impact than trying to flesh out a sentence to make it longer. Simple.

Not everything needs flowering up

Sometimes it's okay to just say it how it is, say it simply, without adding ten tonnes of adjectives to flower it up. If you were talking in real life to Sharon in the bar down the road would everything be stunning? If not, then why is everything in your copy stunning or marvellous? If you are selling a retreat in Ibiza, we know it's going to be pretty spectacular without adding in that it's a "spectacular retreat in Ibiza" or "idyllic Ibiza."

And

Now this is one that's really going to rile the proper English folk. It is completely okay to start a sentence with *and*. I think I might do it quite a lot... But it's because what you are writing needs to feel conversational. Chatty. Real. And whilst we are there it's also okay to start a conversation with but or because.

I wanna get you writing as you speak.

Throw out the dictionary and abbreviate if you need to, to ensure it sounds like you. Because let's face it, if you wanna sound like you oughta then you're gonna have to write like you sound.

CTAs are your friends

When was the last time you asked your audience to do something? It could be to drop an emoji in the comments, asking them to answer a question, getting them to respond to your email or EVEN buy something from you. As entrepreneurs we expect people to respond to us all the time, to interact with our posts, to jump on to our courses but we never ever ask them to do it. I've been guilty of this too so there is no judgement. But if we want them to take action we need to be less fearful of using CTAs (calls to action).

I think the reason we feel this way is because quite honestly we are scared of asking for the sale and always associate CTAs with, "Come buy this from me please." And because we live in an online world where every five minutes we are being sold another thing, we see it as a bit icky. But we can't expect people to buy from us or to do what we want them to do if we never tell them we need them to do something. They haven't got a secret antenna. You are not putting out radio waves. So we must stop our fear of asking our audience to do the thing and make CTAs our friends. Use them regularly. Not just when you sell but in any situation. Ask people their opinions. People are way more likely to buy from you if you have a conversation and engage with them.

Use your voice while you're still finding it

The biggest thing I want you to remember when you are thinking about putting pen to paper is that the first draft of everything is shit. My husband, Rob, is a copywriter and I can't tell you how many times he says to me that he needs to proof-read the work before my eyes even get a peep at it. Why? Because despite it being his career, the first draft always needs fine tuning. It's important to not stifle yourself with trying to create the perfect draft the first time round. It's one of the most common causes of writer's block. We put so much pressure on ourselves for perfection that we end up writing nothing. It's going to take time, you are going to have to refine it. Once, twice, maybe even three times and that is okay. Walk away. Have a cuppa. Refine.

I guess it's about using your voice while you're still finding it. It's like anything in life, you can't wait around for the perfect moment. You might get frustrated that it doesn't sound right. You might read it back and think it's a load of codswallop. But we have to start somewhere. We have to remember that our audience needs to hear what we've got to say. And it may not be the most perfect. It might not be Hemmingway. But it needs to be said. And only when we first get it out on paper, when we first say "the thing" will we know if it worked, if it connected, if it converted. Until we do that how will we ever know?

We are over halfway through this book now and I think it's a good time to check in. Because you have everything you need right inside of you. You have the stories, the words, the connection sitting there waiting to come out. So we can choose to have come this far and forever fear writing the sales page, putting off the social posts or coming out from under the rock we've been hiding under, or we can decide it's time to get ourselves out there.

Because my lovely, you have a chance now to take a step. And yes, you can stay your industry's best kept secret, or we can make now the time to make a change.

13

SAY MY NAME,

SAY MY NAME

I want to start by telling you about an awful cock up I had when I started this brand business and how a clever brand name turned into something that made me cringe for the first year of my business. You see, I'd already named my stationery business after my epic, kick-ass Grandma Betty and something inside me knew I wanted that legacy to carry on. For me to feel like she was connected somehow to my business still. And then it hit me...The B Studio. Such a cool, funky name that not only stood for Brand but also, I knew deep down, stood for Betty.

I loved everything about it and was chuffed to butter-cups when I tried to buy my domain name and it was AVAILABLE. As you know, I always knew I had more to give and it felt like everything was falling into place. I'd written my web copy, had a brand photoshoot, built my website... TOLD the entire internet about it (well, my little corner of it, anyway). Everyone was on board with it and loved it and five days before I was due to go live I hit a hurdle. But this wasn't like a stumbling block, it was a hurdle. Why? Because I couldn't be called The B Studio. Because some other woman, a brand studio no less, was on all the social media channels as MY business name.

Safe to say, I panicked. I'd been telling everyone it was coming. I'd printed gift boxes for big time business coaches and they were ready to send. It couldn't not happen. I couldn't not launch. I'd bigged it up too much. So after many frantic conversations with both my husband and my coach we came to the decision to just keep it simple. Do what it says on the tin. After all, that is just one of the ways you pick a brand name. But with little rational thought and a severe lack of creativity, Branding by Nicki was born. I mean, come on... I am all for simple and to the point but this takes the biscuit. It was like all the creativity had gone and I just had to roll with it.

And the lesson in this is about how important a brand name truly is. I was young, naive and probably a bit oblivious at the time, if I am honest, and one bad mistake was something I had to live with every single day as I introduced myself as Nicki from Branding by Nicki. That's not even Ronseal, that's a B&Q basic right there. I'd love to say it stopped there but Branding by Nicki transformed to B by Nicki when I realised it wasn't just stereotypical "branding" that I did. I didn't want to do a complete overhaul as I felt known by this point so just "randing" disappeared. And with that came an array of Google search problems because if you searched B by Nicki you had an SEO battle with Nicky Minaj. Or a youth text message spelling of baby. But then one day I had a lightbulb moment. I noticed more and more that I was always saying, be you and that you had all the power you needed within you and we shouldn't be anyone else: we should Just Brand You™. And so it was born. My little Ronseal name, but with huge impact. Safe to say, I trademarked that one, checked it was available everywhere and now it's a huge part of everything I do.

So after many failed attempts it taught me all of what was important when picking your brand name and I want to keep it simple for you. There are three ways to nail your brand name and it certainly isn't with a B&Q basics.

What it is on the tin

You heard me say in Chapter Two that Donald Millar famously says, "People are drawn towards clarity and away from confusion," and this is the exact same for your brand name too. Sometimes people spend so long trying to be so clever with it but actually it's sitting there staring you in the face. So, similarly to my Just Brand You, think about what you say a lot or what you do and find a creative twist to it. The benefits? People easily understand what you do, you will find it easier to be found on Google and in fact any other search engine but most importantly your clients will easily recognise your service.

Your name

As I am sure you are starting to catch on now, as small business owners people buy from us and who we are. And we can't hide behind any aspects of our brands. So especially for the service-based readers, just simply using your name could suffice. We don't always have to overcomplicate this. Think of how many coaches you know who just use their name. They do it for a reason. Because you could have the fanciest business name in the world and it could be seriously cool but the likelihood is if you are a service based business people are still going to refer to you as your name, as a woman, rather than a business. So if in doubt, your name has clout.

No fancy name without reason

I bet you've seen so many business names all over the internet and half of them give you no clear idea as to why they are called it. And the best bit is when they don't even have a reason for calling it what they have. As an example, say you have a name of Tallulah Kitchens and you are a kitchen manufacturer and people go, "Oh, why Tallulah?" and you have to turn round and go, "Dunno! I just liked it!" You are going to feel a bit silly, right? So if you are going to go for a name that is a fancy word, or something a little more obscure, ensure it has meaning to you. Ensure there is a way that you can storytell around why you've picked it. Perhaps it's one of your children's names, somewhere you used to live, a memory, an emotional feeling. But something that gives it rhyme and reason. This brand name is going to encapsulate everything that you do and a name you like just because it sounds pretty at the time may not have the same emotion when it goes out of trend two years later.

What do you do if you are changing your name?

Now, I need to make it clear that it is completely and utterly okay to change your business name if you are reading this chapter and realised that the name of your business just ain't cutting it anymore. I've changed my business name twice now. And I am not saying that you should yo-yo around changing it every five minutes but our businesses are always going to grow, the services we offer change and we might find ourselves at a pivotal crossroads where the name just doesn't work for us anymore and that is okay. We are not signing on the dotted line and vowing to never change it. But we do have to be clever when we do change it. It's not just as simple as doing your rebrand and changing it over. You should use this change in your business to connect with your clients, ask them their thoughts and opinions, tell them what you are doing. Don't just wake up one day, change your social handles and go *ta-dah!* Take them on the journey with you. And not just for your business name change but every part of the brand journey. Talk to them about your decisions, tell them your reasonings and let them be part of your business with you.

14

YOUR SHOP WINDOW

"You don't need a website." Words I've heard come out of people's lips on many occasions in the online space. And if I am honest, it's true. You don't NEED one. Back in the day I used to get so frustrated when I'd see coaches I truly admired saying this. I'd never say anything but I'd get in a huff and complain to the hubby, deep down panicking that it would stop people coming to me for my services. But now I have to say part of them is right. Now... You might think I am a bit barmy saying you don't *need* a website when essentially one of the things I provide for my clients are websites but hear me out, let me explain...

Every single brand needs a platform. A shop window. A place to sell. That can be on a social media page, that can be on an online platform such as Kartra or Kajabi but the further along you get on your journey, the more likely you are to need more ways for people to find you and a place where you can showcase your brand. Your website becomes a place where people go to find out more about what you do. They can find out more about you as a person and how you can best serve them and it gives you an awful lot of brand recognition and kudos. It's an elevation tool. And when used correctly your website can become a money-making machine.

Think of it as your shop window. A really, really good shop window. Like Selfridges. With the best window displays that people go out of their way just to see when on Oxford Street, London. It gives you that sneak peek as to the magic that awaits inside. It gets you excited and it becomes a work of art on its own.

But I do have to admit that I understand why people say that you don't need one. Because not everyone treats their website with the care it deserves. Not everyone uses it the way it should be used and not everyone understands how to make their website work harder. And without knowing those things you may as well not have a website. See, a website with just pretty pictures on it is exactly that. A website with pretty pictures on it. But a website that works, that considers the way it speaks to its viewer, that considers all of the things its viewer needs and that takes its viewer on a journey with them is powerful. And one better than that is a website that gets found because it offers the exact information that the viewer needs and so they stumble upon it while doing their internet surfing. Well, that is groundbreaking.

So we need to start treating our websites as our show-case. For online businesses they are our hub. Our shop window display that makes people want to take the leap and find out more. It's the difference between client confusion and client realisation. And it most definitely should be a platform you are pushing every-thing you do back to.

If it's good, it'll do 80-90% of the selling for you

It's true. A good, well turned-out website can get your clients falling in love with you. It can get them thinking you are the best thing since sliced bread. I want to take you back to Chapter Nine, where I spoke about how no one likes a Selly Sally. Well, let's reposition that for a second. We know we don't like continuously being sold to. But also one of the biggest things stopping entre-preneurs getting ahead is that they are scared to ask for the sale. They clam up the second they have to "pitch." You know, when you have someone enquire about your services? Most people are probably going to get them on a discovery call to make sure they are the right fit, right? Just to make sure there are no huge clashes. And then the panic sets in... "I am going to have to justify what I do." "I am going to have to divulge my prices... Am I worth it?" And we fear the call. We go into it worrying that we are going to have to sell ourselves and our services.

So let's imagine it didn't have to be that way. That the call could become a friendly conversation just to make sure you like each other. That it would be like chatting to a friend rather than nervous sweats about whether or not they are going to buy. Well, how can that happen? I hear you ask. Well, your website has already done that hard work for you.

And don't just take my word for it. I want you to truly understand the power your website has and you are going to understand that a lot more from hearing about the results than you are from me banging on for 50,000 words. Let me introduce you to Viv Guy. Now, I am not saying at all that we didn't put a LOT of work in on all the other chapters up until now but I kid you not, Viv's website is one of the most mentioned websites when I ask for what their brand inspiration is, that I've ever done. People love it. It feels like Viv, it sounds like Viv, it looks like Viv. And she talks to her audience and she shows her audience exactly why they need her in their lives. It's not just a few words on a page and a pretty picture or two. Don't get me wrong, it looks great but it's all the considered elements that truly get across what Viv is trying to achieve, that made it a money-making machine. And not after months and months of getting found on Google (although that is important). It took Viv precisely one day, nope, not even one day, half a day, to get four new bookings.

Viv came to me with a very strong idea of what she offered in her business. As a photographer (at the time) Viv specialised in many areas: brand, portrait, boudoir, family, weddings... the list goes on! But despite her niching based on her very moody (and EPIC) photography style something just wasn't quite sitting right. We found ourselves in many conversations about how she was going to speak to all of these people. After all, as you know, your brand has to look, feel and sound like you but also (and most importantly) speak to your ideal client. Well, she just had so many!

Social media was going to be tricky and designing a site that encompassed all of her varied skill sets was a difficult task. But one of course that we managed to deliver on. But still, there was that niggling feeling and I could just tell that Viv wasn't happy. So the day she came to me and opened up and suddenly the decision was made that Viv was going to be "THE personal brand photographer in the North", I think we both breathed a sigh of relief. And from there we completely changed the website. Started again. To make sure we had it completely right.

See, the reason I am telling you this is because too many people overcomplicate their websites. They overcomplicate their services and pile on more and more to offer something for everyone. They overcomplicate their homepage. They overcomplicate the entire thing full stop. So we stripped back completely what Viv was doing. Niched her down, thought about what her ideal client needed to hear, what they needed to know and teamed that with some of Viv's sassiness (a classic photographer's nightmare of bending over in jeans to get the perfect shot and showing some of your bum crack - Yep! That featured on there) and we spoke to her audience through her website in a way that only she could. It was really Viv. And people loved it. They bought into it. She had a fresh perspective. She was doing something different.

But the biggest trick was that it was considered. All of the elements of not just what makes a good website but what makes a good brand. And it paid off. She became spoken about. She was seen everywhere. People loved what she offered and landed on her website and converted. Her brand did 80-90% of the selling for it. The clients just came!

And the best bit? It wasn't just the clients rolling in. It was the spark and light coming back to Viv's eyes, because she was doing something she loved. She could now go out there with something she was proud of and it's that inner confidence that makes that website a must have. That's the power of a brand...

Viv Guy

And I want you to have the same results. I want you to know the things you need to consider. It's what this entire book is all about. So over the next few sections I am going to give you some actionable tips to make sure that your website is working that little bit harder. To show you some of the things that you need to be considering, to have a website that does that selling for you too.

It's about painting a picture

I can't tell you how many websites I see out there that just don't cut it. It's like we expect our clients to guess what we do or just know what it's like to work with us. A well-converting website doesn't make people guess. It shows them. You see, it's about painting a picture. Setting the scene. I guess it's just like reading a book. It's about getting people to hear your voice as they are reading your copy, getting them to feel your personality as they look through your photography. Getting them to understand the journey they would embark on if they worked with you and the results they would have. Let's pretend we are wedding planners. Well, any wedding planner can go, "I can help you plan your wedding. Here are my services; full plan, part plan, event plan" but only YOU can talk to them about the magic of working with you. Only you can show them why you are the person they need.

It's about thinking bigger here. It's about using all of those tips from Chapter Twelve and bringing them to this. It's about answering all of their worries. Showing you are inside their head and get it. It's about using some of their language and showing you understand. It's not about the top line. It's about showing them both visually and in writing about who you are and what you offer. It's not about dipping the toe in the water and telling them a little bit. It's about opening up your business and spilling it onto your website. Not waffling. Not jargon. You. Your business. And most importantly them.

Tell them where to go

Now, I don't think a good website is a place to tell your viewers where to go in the slightly rude sense. Although we don't want it to appeal to everyone, of course. That's why we define our ideal client. But this has a slightly different meaning of telling them where to go. When you are looking at your website and the pages of your website you need to think about the hot pages you want them to go to. The pages with your services or portfolio on as an example. We can't just assume that our clients are going to be able to find them or know that's where you eventually want them to land. We have to tell them. And tell them really, really clearly. You almost need to treat your viewer a bit like a dummy. Like they've landed on Mars and have zero clue how to work their way around.

A few ways to think about this is with things such as clear navigation menus. That's like your home, about, work with me, etc. Essentially, your buttons to get them around the site. Here is not a time to be fancy. We don't want obscure or fancy names. We need to keep it as easy for the customer as possible.

Secondly, CTAs or calls to action, are your friends. Your best friends. And a call to action is crucial for your website. It's a way for you to be able to have a teensy bit more control of where your viewer goes. We can't assume that people will click around on your website the same way you do. So we have to guide them. You want to make sure that before the fold - before a user has to scroll at all, that you have a clear call to action taking them to a key page. This normally redirects to your services page or sometimes, if you are a creative business, your portfolio. It's a chance for them to find out more. But it doesn't just end there. These CTAs need to be dotted around your website at key places where you need them to take action. And not just one per page. At every point you want them to do something. They don't have to be boring either and they certainly don't all have to say *find out more*. Think of little phrases you would use that make your person-ality shine and that make you easily identifiable.

It only takes a minute, girl

Well, actually three seconds. That is exactly how long you have from when someone lands on your website to when they decide whether to stick around or not. That is barely any time at all. So what you put right at the top of your homepage is crucial. You want to have key statements. Perhaps even your brand message up there. You want an image or imagery that showcases either who you are or what you do and you need a visible and clear logo so people know where they've landed. Now, I know that last point sounds stupid. They've clicked on your website right. But what happens if traffic to your website didn't only come from social media? Where they knew exactly whose website they were clicking through to? What happens if something epic happened and they found you on the magic that is Google? I don't know about you, but I click around Google faster than you can say Just Brand You. So the person might not always know where they've landed. We want to tell them.

Because all of business and let's face it, even life, is about first impressions. We judge people so quickly. We make assumptions and we have to assume that's what our audience is doing too. That's why those three seconds count. 'Cos if they click off, they ain't coming back. And you've lost them forever. What a waste that is.

52 blogs a year

Whilst we are talking about people finding you through Google, I wanted to touch based on the 52 blogs you should be writing every year. It sounds like a lot, but honestly it's one a week and it needs to be part of your brand strategy if you want your website to work for you. I've seen so many people complain that their websites aren't converting but they haven't changed a single thing on it since 2018! Let me give you a quick tip on how Google is going to find your website and show it to people without going down the SEO worm-hole too much. We'll leave that to the whizzkids. Google shows your website to people who type in questions or phrases and you answer the content or use the phrases within your website. It trawls the internet daily, probably millisecondly (made up word, I know) looking for keywords based on people's searches. So if your website has zero new content then where do you think your website is going to show up?

But it isn't just about getting found. Having a great blog with tonnes of content whether written or even a video blog (or a vlog as it's also known) will give you another platform to show your clients your expertise. You will be able to use it as a tool for social media too as it will help with additional content and you can use allllll of those ideal client pain points that you've found out from Chapter Four and answer them all. Then when you sit down and plan your week's social content you can tick off one day because you've got a blog to go out. Then you can tick off another because you could pull a quote from it. You with me?

Imagine if you found one website from one epic lady who completely just got you. Like they could dig into your brain and answer all of your thoughts and feelings. You are going to buy from them, right? You are going to want their solution, right?

And remember these don't have to be complicated or six thousand word essays. It could be as simple as five top tips on a subject. Or a mini-story about something. Or even a spotlight on a client. So there is no excuse to not blog. Make it non-negotiable if your website is a hub for everything you do. Start now... you need at least one this week!

If it looks poop on mobile then it ain't working

I am really nervous that this subsection might get a bit ranty. If it does, I apologise. When was the last time you checked your analytics on your social media platform? Have you ever checked your analytics on your social media platforms? If not, why not? You need to be doing that regularly, because I am intrigued to know how many times people click through to your websites from your social channels. I guess for most of you that is probably where your clients are finding you. So imagine you are scrolling through that beautiful feed of yours crammed full of great content and they decide it's time to find out more. Now, most of us scroll on our phones. We live in a generation where it's permanently glued to our hip, so we have to expect that most people are looking at our websites... you guessed it... on their phones! So why, please tell me why, does everyone ONLY concentrate on how beautiful their website looks on desktop and give up with how mobile displays?

The way your website looks on mobile is just as important if not more important than desktop. Because you could have the fanciest desktop website but if the majority of your visitors are coming from their iPhone and half the copy is cut off or you only have one eyeball and half a nostril then it's not working for you. And you could well be leaving good money on the table. So you must, must be checking mobile first. It must become a priority and if it ain't looking right or you've got fancy pants sliders or gizmos on it that don't work on mobile then that needs to be fixed. Don't allow yourself to lose customers because you didn't put mobile first.

IN YOUR BRAND JOURNAL

Let's do a little test. Head on to your website and make sure you've got all of these things present and correct.

1. Clear statements or your brand message that sit before the user has to scroll.

2. Imagery that shows either you or showcases what you do that doesn't leave you with half an eyeball.

3. A visible logo - No small little dot, please - thank you!

4. A clear call to action to tell people where you want them to go before the fold and then several throughout the website.

5. An easy to use navigation or menu without fancy pants words that helps people get around the site.

6. A good mobile design that doesn't crop off half of the content.

7. A blog answering all of your clients' pain points and questions.

I want to leave you with one last tip to summarise the chapter. Start using your website as an important marketing tool for your brand so you can stop pulling your hair out making a sale. Let it do the hard work for you.

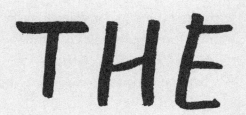

THE

So we've hit another milestone and that can only mean one thing. We need another checklist to make sure you know exactly what we've covered in this book and what you need to start considering for becoming your brand.

THE INSPIRATION

1. First off, we have to remember that when everyone else that does what we do zigs, we need to zag. It's about looking at your industry and making sure we are not doing anything similar.
2. We need to head over to Pinterest, or in magazines, packaging, EVERYWHERE and find inspiration for our new brand identity. Remember, we are breaking this into inspiration for: your logos, your websites, colours, patterns or textures, fonts and even your brand photography. Remember to look outside of your industry.
3. We need to create an overall mood board after really refining down all of our inspiration.

THE BRAND IDENTITY

1. We need to organise a photoshoot and scout out our photographers. Remember we are not going for the stereotypical. Think about where you'd hang out and what is truly reflective of your brand.
2. You are going to use your inspiration to find all of your fonts and start putting together your three piece suite of

RECAP

logos. A primary logo, alternative logo and a submark. Make sure that whatever you are doing, whether yourself or someone else is designing this, that you have your twist on it.

3. You are going to be picking your colour palette, looking for 2-3 main colours and maximum three additional secondary colours.

THE COPY

1. It's time to analyse your current copy or to start crafting new copy. Remember, the first draft of everything is shit, so keep at it and speak from the heart.

2. Remember to refine it and then just put it out. It's better to use your voice while still finding it than say nothing at all.

YOUR BRAND NAME

1. Now this one isn't for everyone. There is a chance you won't need to change your brand name but remember the three rules.

        a. What it is on the tin

        b. Your name

        c. Or something fancy but only with a reason for it being there

1. Start with thinking about where you want your client to go on your website. Think about the key pages that hold the information that will make people want to work with you. Usually, your home, services, portfolio/testimonials.

2. Make sure that above the fold (before your audience has to scroll) you have all of the elements you need. Remember you've got three seconds.

3. Get blogging. One a week to be precise.

4. Double and triple check mobile and iPad as well as desktop.

It's now time to live this brand. This is my favourite part as it's all about to take shape and it's where you can make the biggest impact with your brand. Buckle in, because things are about to get real.

LIVE BRAND YOU ⟶

LIVE
BRAND
YOU

15

THE COMING OUT PARTY

Bloomin' 'eck! Fifteen chapters deep and I think I've truly "Lived Brand You" myself. Either that or levelled up to a completely new part of my brand. You see, writing this book was just another step in my journey. Another thing I needed to do in order to continue growing. Because your brand grows with you every single day and in order for it to be its most effective you have to live it. Look after it. Respect it. You have to embody it. You have to be it. And you have to allow it space to grow. As well as showing the hell up. But more of that in the next chapter.

Everything we've spoken about until now is part of working out who you are and bringing that to life. But you can't just put this book down at the end of the website chapter and hope for the best that you are going to have clients lining up at your door and suddenly be number one in your field. It just doesn't work that way. We have to get people speaking about us, we have to create a "thing," or lots of "things" in fact and we have to keep making noise until people hear us. That is what living brand you is all about. Not hitting pause at this crucial moment. Which you will be surprised is super common. But that's where people fall short. They think they are done and in fact it's only just getting started. It's about carrying on and, as the title of this chapter suggests, hosting your own coming out party. Announcing all of this epic work you've done on your brand and showcasing it to the world. It's time ladies... We are going to step into that unfamiliar woman now.

You're ready.

Falling trees.

I want to take you back again to my first business, Betty Lou Design. Back when I had zero clue about how I was going to get seen and heard. When I had an idea for a business and was doing the 9-5/entrepreneurial juggle. Back to a time when more than anything I wanted it to work out. To be a business owner. I wanted to design stationery for tonnes of clients, make all the money and look back and wonder how I'd come so far. I expected instant results. And I made more mistakes in those first few months than I have ever since. It's a bit ironic really that when I started out I was trying to attract everyone, but actually if I look back now to the way that I launched, it's not surprising I attracted no one.

I'd followed all the steps, created the logo, made the website, opened the Facebook and Instagram channels, left them dormant for a good few weeks, followed a few people the day before my launch, created a couple of hashtag bundles and then *ta-dah!* Here is Betty Lou Design. Website was live. A social post announcing I was open went out. No traffic to the website. I got about five visitors and I bet half of those were my Mum. But I can't be surprised really, can I?

Because it's like that famous philosophical quote: "If a tree falls in a forest and no one is around to hear it, does it make a sound?" It's so poignant for brands, especially at the time of showcasing them to the world. If you don't shout about it, how do you expect anyone to know about it? It needs to be a damn sight more than one pretty post on Instagram. There needs to be a strategy behind it. A purpose.

Create a "thing"

It's time to think about your launch plan. We need to make as much noise as we possibly can to get your ideal client and all of your industry peers shouting about you from the rooftops. We need people to take notice. To celebrate with you. But to do that we need a strategy. And this can't just be a few posts on social media. We want to get maximum impact from this. It might be a live event or series, it could be something in person, it could be sending out gifts to industry people, it could be getting local PR or building new connections but you want to find a way that not only you will be shouting about it but others will too.

Creating a launch plan for your brand needs to be bigger than just you shouting about it once. It needs to be you giving something to your audience. It can't just be, "Hey, look at me, come and give this post some love." What's the incentive? Why do they want to come and check out your new brand? What's in it for them? Are you going to teach them something? Is there a new limited time offering that is only available during launch? It's time to get creative here. It's time to use your business brain and think of how you can get maximum results.

Make it your time to shine

This is your springboard. A chance for you to make an impact and show your audience that you have arrived. It's the first step on the ladder of living brand you and it's about you putting your flag in the sand. It's about that dial finally being turned up and you owning who you were meant to be. You've done the work... that's the hard bit. Now it's about starting your visibility journey and continuing to show up every single day. This isn't the end. This is only the beginning.

So what happens next? The launch is done. It was a fabulous success and you gained lots of attraction and it's at this point people keep up the visibility for a month or so and then they give up. Because it takes time, because it's yet another thing to do on a never ending to do list to grow your business. And it's the scariest thing. So it's the first to go. But if you actually think it's a lot less about you and a lot more about them, and remember that by not consistently showing up for your audience you are actually doing them a disservice, you'll soon realise that it needs to be a core part of your strategy from now on.

There is no such thing as miracles

I always get asked how I got this far and how I did it so fast. As if some miracle occurred and I had a secret ingredient that no one else had. Well, yes, that's kind of true. I do have things that others don't. Of course I do. But as we know, you have that too. So how did I jump ahead and become a multi-six-figure entrepreneur in just a few short years? It all came down to consistency with visibility. Showing up continuously with posts, in Facebook groups (not just my own), speaking about my expertise in others' group programs and courses, live videos; you name it, I'm doing it. Because I realised that if I didn't then I wasn't going to get seen. There is no such thing as overnight success. There is no such thing as flicking a switch and becoming a successful entrepreneur. It takes hard work, dedication and drive. And it isn't for everyone. I don't even think you'd be this far into this book if you thought you didn't need a bit of elbow grease to make this happen.

But it needs to be consistent. It's not a try this one day and then give up because it didn't get the results that you wanted. I want to introduce you now to Mrs Pringle. And she is a perfect example of the classic tagline *once you pop you just can't stop*. I use her every single time as a teaching tool when someone tells me they don't want to show up in their business, or make excuses for why they can't. Because she is a classic example of how if you are not consistent the results won't be the same.

Mrs Pringle came to me when she'd reached a bit of a low point. She'd been grafting and grafting and struggling to reap the rewards of all her hard work. Mrs Pringle owned a bridal boutique and despite it being absolutely beautiful and her having clients and a small team of staff, Mrs Pringle hadn't paid herself or taken a wage for years. She knew something needed to change but she didn't know what. She knew that she couldn't carry on with a business that, even though she loved it more than anything in the world, wasn't serving her financially.

During our time together we worked on some key areas to decipher why we weren't hitting the targets in the business that would allow Mrs Pringle to take a wage home. And one of the biggest things was to increase her visibility. So we set tasks and discussed strategies on how we could start showing more than just pretty dress pictures and more of herself and her team into their social feeds. After all, we all know people buy from people and what I am about to tell you is proof that it doesn't matter whether your business is product or service-based, that you can scale your business to where you want it to be once people start to see your face. Within a few months of working together and consistently showing up for her audience, Mrs Pringle made a whopping £30,000 month and better yet, they kept on coming. And Mrs Pringle finally took a wage. I was so happy.

Now as with all things, our time had to come to an end. Our program finished, our time together was done, but Mrs Pringle had all she needed to keep up these results. A few months later I received a text message that the boutique wasn't making the same results and she'd gone back to not taking a wage. She couldn't understand why. But you know the one thing that changed? Mrs Pringle stopped showing up. She'd gone back to the pretty pictures on her pretty feed and wasn't showing the person or people in this case behind it.

Mrs Pringle

ONCE YOU
POP YOU
JUST CAN'T
STOP

PRINGLES

———

So what is the lesson here? Why do I need you to take this in? It's because in business, with our brands, if we stop and I'm not just talking for a day here and there or even a week, I mean a month and then two months and so on, then you may as well start again. Your clients are looking forward to hearing from you. And if you aren't going to show up for them, then someone else will. Every time you show up for your audience is another step closer to them wanting to work with you. But if you're not there, showing them you are ready, then they'll go to the person who is. So keep up the consistency. Make sure no matter how polished or perfect it is that you are using your voice while you find it.

It's okay to be a bit ranty pants

It's time to speak from the heart. It might not always be a lesson or a teaching you want to shout about. Don't be afraid to talk about things in your industry that frustrate you or something you've heard on the news that's created a spark inside you. We need to start thinking of showing up to our audience, just like we would chat with our friends and just relax with it. No one is waiting for you to slip up. No one is going to tell you off if you slip an F* bomb in there now again. And no one is going to judge you for having opinions. It's completely and utterly okay to get a bit ranty pants. In fact, I encourage it.

Some of my most powerful live videos with the best engagement are ones where I say it how it is. Now, I am not saying you need to call people out or do this in a nasty way. Everything should be done with love, but the only way you are going to stand out is if you challenge situations. If you are prepared to share your passions and start a conversation. It's going to be these things that your client relates with. You are gonna have to make some noise to be heard. Having a business isn't a time to be quiet. So it's about taking consistent action to get you to where you want to be. Because remember, if you ain't shouting about it, no one else will.

16

YOU WILL NEVER BE THE FIRST

Now... I need to tell you something and it's really important. You will never be the first to do what you do or teach what you teach. I am aware that sounds a bit mean but it's the truth. And we've been together now for goodness knows how many pages so I am hoping you know I am saying this with love. This isn't my attempt at telling you that all your incredible ideas aren't unique. They can be. And they will be. But we will always have gained our knowledge from somewhere, been inspired by something or heard something and wanted to share it with our audience. And that is completely okay. No one is coming up with anything completely and utterly new.

I wasn't the first person to talk about all of these elements of brand building. They've been going for decades. I will totally admit that I got inspired about who my ideal client was by a business coach I followed. I openly admit that I haven't always had that down. But I never wanted to teach it in the same way. I never wanted to steal someone else's content because that's not cool. But we would never say anything if we always thought we needed to come up with some new revolutionary idea every time.

The difference and lesson here is how we make it our own. I am sure you've seen people complaining on social media about people stealing content and copying. No one wants to be called out for that and let me be clear that isn't okay. But you are going to grow in your business and with that you will listen to things and find your own ways to utilise them and make them your own. And one of the best ways to do that is through storytelling. Creating your own unique content that puts your own twist on what you teach is a huge part of living brand you. It's what makes you stand out and it can give your audience the chance to finally understand what you are trying to teach and have that penny drop moment even though they may have heard it from others many times. The time they hear it from you, in your way, it finally sinks in. And that is powerful, because once you help someone and they see a change, they are much more likely to buy from you.

So why is storytelling so important? Let's think about this differently. I don't know about you, but when I was younger, one of my favourite times of day was bedtime. Strange, I know, as this is usually most children's worst nightmare. But for me it was a special time with my Mum getting engrossed into the latest story we were reading. Our imagination as children is just phenomenal. It's amazing how we can take ourselves to that different place. Imagine ourselves as the princess in the castle or a fish swimming in the big ocean. The lessons we learn from the words people write on pages has always fascinated me. But I think sometimes we forget that the imagination we had as children doesn't just disappear as adults. We maybe don't quite use it in the same way anymore: I mean, I no longer dress up as a fairy princess but I do find a good story or a new way for me to visualise something a hugely helpful tool in order for me to understand a concept. It gives me a chance to get excited about it. And let's face it, in business we all need a bit more magic in our lives.

So when we are teaching our audience all we can really do is add our twist on it, because there is no new news.

It's time we opened our eyes to inspiration

So where do we find this information? How do we start to put our own twist on things? Well, it's honestly easier than you think if you just open your eyes to what is happening around you. If you truly start to listen to the conversations you have with your clients, business besties or even just your pals. Because inspiration is absolutely everywhere. But we spend so much time with our blinkers on, concentrating on the thing in hand, that we shut out the incredible things happening around us.

Your stories can come from all manner of things. Let's start with the obvious... It could be as simple as utilising part of your business journey, or an experience you've had in your life that can explain what you want people to help people to understand. But it can be more than that. It could be a television program, a song lyric, a moment in time when you are engrossed and inspired. I've got inspiration down the local pub listening to some blokes giving each other jib about the football on the telly. It's all around us.

Now don't be sitting there, reading this and saying, it's okay for you because you know how to do this. When did you last really listen to your favourite series on Netflix? When did you last take in the words and immerse yourself in it? Rather than playing on your phone at the same time? One of my favourite bits of inspiration is from the opening scene in my fave medical drama New Amsterdam. Where the medical director Max Goodwin (helps that he's hot) stands in front of all the department heads and asks one simple question, "How can I help?" they all stare back at him in amazement because they'd never been asked that before. They were always told what to do, when to do it, how to do it.

And in that moment a lightbulb went on in my head. How often do we actually ask our audience this question? We spend so long thinking we know what they need, putting out offer after offer hoping that they will jump at it, but we never ask the simple question that will mean that we are actually going to offer them something they want. We don't listen. When did you last just ask?

How much stronger is it to paint a picture around it rather than to just say, "Stop getting frustrated they ain't buying your thing and bloomin' well ask them."

I realise it's easy for me to talk about it. But I want to give you an example of probably one of my most well received emails that summarises how this plays out in real life. It didn't come from anywhere special. I was on a little UK break and if I am honest, I was going to be a bit naughty and skip the weekly email as I'd been so relaxed and not thinking about work that I hadn't given it a thought. We'd arrived in this beautiful little pub on top of a cliff overlooking the sea and it hit me. Just there, in that moment.

> Today I am going to compare us all to seagulls. At the moment I'm away in Kent and we've visited so many seaside towns and I've never felt so relaxed. You see, I was brought up by the sea and there is something so calming about being back to my roots. The sound of the sea, the sand between your toes and the sun kissing your face. It's given me so much thinking space, so many ideas and I've truly cleared my head, ready for some pretty exciting plans for Q4.

Anyway, I digress because what I want to say is that we should all be a little more like a seagull. As I sat here with my glass of Sauvignon Blanc (I wrote this yesterday) I just watched and gazed at them gliding through the air. It's so graceful, which is hilarious when you think of their notorious, cheeky traits that I've decided to describe them as graceful.

However, if you think about it, they glide through life without a care in the world and they dive when they want or when they need to. They don't go into it half-hearted, or half-arsed, they go for it full pelt. There's no hesitation, no second thoughts. They see the prize, they focus, they keep their eye on it and they get what they want. It's almost unapologetic. They have gumption.

And I think we need to take a little bit of inspiration from them. Now, I'm not telling you to go around stealing people's chips (that would just be rude) but I am saying that we need to stop being fearful about what we want. Glide when you need to and enjoy the ride and then dive in headfirst to what you need to do to get what you want. Be fearless. Be brave. And don't let anything stop you.

Be more seagull.

See? So you can even sit there having a cheeky glass of vino and the inspiration will come. And sometimes you don't even know why an experience is relevant. What its purpose is. But you know it's got something. I like to keep a note on my phone of things. So even if they don't seem relevant at the time, I can reflect on them. Come back to them when I know there's something I want to say but I am not sure how to say it. There'll always be something in that bank of gems, I promise!

Now it's time to start thinking about how we actually craft these posts...

Remember the seven basic plot twists I told you about when telling your story. Well, you can use these plot twists for your storytelling content too. It might help you with things you should be looking out for or ways you can take something that has inspired you and how you add the story element to it.

BE MORE
SEAGULL

GLIDE WHEN YOU NEED TO AND ENJOY THE RIDE

AND THEN DIVE IN HEADFIRST TO WHAT YOU NEED

TO DO TO GET WHAT YOU WANT.

BE FEARLESS. BE BRAVE.

AND DON'T LET ANYTHING STOP YOU.

So how do we tell these stories and use this content?

Well, quite simply you need to be speaking to your audience every, single day. And storytelling content must be a part of that. There are no excuses. It's time to knock down that fifty foot wall now that you are hiding behind.

But the good thing is, I've got you. I've got a super simple formula that helps you to craft your bit of inspiration and turn it into a post that your audience are going to love. I like to think of it as a roller coaster.

The Start - Where all the anticipation happens. You are on the up and you are setting the scene. Here is where I want you to tell the actual story. What did you hear, see or experience?

The Middle - The loop-dee loop. Or the main crux of the story. Here is where you are going to add your twist on the story. It's where you are going to tell them the reason as to why you are telling this story. It's the message or the lesson we all need to learn from this story.

The End - When you get to the end of the ride and you have that weird moment of calm and then the buzz to do it all over again. Here is where we put the transformation or solution for your clients. Like my "it's time we were all a bit more seagull and dived for what we wanted." This is the empowering moment, where you can add your call to action. What do you want them to do next?

There is always more

Now, of course I don't want you thinking you need to tell stories every single day. Because you don't. And I am not sitting here saying I am a content expert but when it comes to the posts you are putting up that relate to your brand I like to break mine into three key categories. Storytelling content, talking to my ideal clients' pain points to show them you get it and are listening and analogy content (which we all know by now I love to use). But really good content comes down to trial and error. There is no one stop shop, or a secret formula. It's about being honest, true and real and finding what works for you. What gets your clients connecting. And taking them on the journey with you.

Remember, it's all about relatability being a stand-out brand. Don't try to be above people. Stand on their level, speak to them your way and you'll be much more likely to grow at the pace you set. Now... where are those raving cheerleaders?

THE START

Where all the anticipation happens. You are setting the scene. Here is where I want you to tell the actual story. What did you hear, see or experience?

THE MIDDLE

The main crux of the story. Here is where you are going to add your twist on the story. It's where you are going to tell them the reason as to why you are telling this story. It's the message or the lesson we all need to learn from this story.

THE END

Here is where we put the transformation or solution for your clients. This is the empowering moment, where you can add your call to action. What do you want them to do next?

17

RAVING CHEERLEADERS
ON SPEED

Treat your people well. Reap the rewards later. Well, as well as doing it just because you are a good person too.

Raving Cheerleaders is one of the most crucial chapters of living brand you. I've saved the best 'til last. Because there are two types of cheerleader. The client who has experienced the journey with you who is going to shout about you from the rooftops, and also that loyal tribe of followers who hang off every word you say and are really attracted to what you've got to say. You've heard the saying "your vibe attracts your tribe", right? And if you spend enough time nurturing and engaging with the people who follow you, giving them tips, advice and actually getting to know them as human beings as well as a number then they will be a lot more likely to become a customer later down the line.

I like to think of it as positioning myself at their level. I see too many entrepreneurs see themselves as part of a hierarchy. Because they know more about one particular subject they almost put themselves on a pedestal.

And don't get me wrong, it's great if your audience looks up to you and are inspired by you but it needs to come from them and not you. We can't sit there looking down on people who don't know what we know.

Yes, they want to learn from us, but I want to introduce you to a new concept that's about stepping down off of the platform and standing with your audience. Speaking to them about how business isn't always sunshine and roses. Speaking to them about hurdles you've overcome. Not being afraid to admit you don't know every single thing and actually acknowledging that they can teach you too. A great person once said, "To be an expert you need to know more about a subject than anyone else in the room." And they are right. So think of it this way... Every single person in your audience is an expert on their subject. More of an expert than you. And they might want to learn your knowledge but to grow raving cheerleaders we need to not think we are the bee's knees.

Be a bit humble now and again.

We've also got to show them all of that Define Brand You work, all of those passion messages so they can see the real you inside. These guys become your squad. They pick you up when you are down, they want you to have success and they'll polish your crown when it needs a bit more sparkle. These people are going to eventually become your customers so looking after them now is crucial. Not just waiting 'til they become a pound sign in your bank.

Building raving cheerleaders starts now.

But there's also another type of cheerleader

Because one of the best ways to build your brand is to work on the tribe of cheerleaders who've already worked with you and love you. You know, the clients who absolutely rave about you, so you don't always have to toot your own horn. Word of mouth is huge for brand reputation and it's the results, experience and connection that your clients feel that makes them want to tell their friends about you. And word of mouth gets you more clients inevitably and then you are in the cycle where they tell their friends and so on. And the best bit is that when you absolutely HATE showing up and giving it the "sell" because it feels icky and makes you cringe, you don't need to worry. Because they are gonna get shouting and letting people know that it is a no brainer and that they need you in their back pockets.

BUILDING
RAVING
CHEERLEADERS

STARTS NOW

———

You see, it's easy to say you are good. It's easy to say you can help but it's the testimonials and cheerleaders that push people over the line. But it's not even just asking for a good testimonial, although you should be doing that as standard practice. It's when all of your past clients come out of the woodwork to spur you on when you need it most that you know you've done a good job. When they start commenting on all of the posts about how game changing it is to work with you. And when you've done your job right, you don't even need to ask them to do it for you. These people will be so connected to who you are and the game changing experience they had that it will be second nature. They want to see you succeed. Because let's face it, business is all about connection and giving each other a leg up when they need it most. And the more that pops up, the more likely new people will see it.

It's all about the customer journey

Your brand is just as much about the people who you've already secured as much as it is building a new audience of people who may or may not want to buy from you.

And this doesn't need to be insanely difficult.

If you spend enough time concentrating on the people you work with once you've secured them, going the extra mile now and again and under promising but over delivering, your cheerleaders will naturally appear. You've got the knowledge. You know you want to help people. Now it's about showing them it, taking them on a journey and making sure they absolutely love it.

So we have to think of our brands from right when our client first finds us, all the way through to checking in with them after a project is done to see how they are getting on. Because it's in all the small details that they remember why they came to you. It's about showing up for them. Being focused when you are with them and delivering them the best possible service. It's about considering all of the details, from how they know exactly what is going on to ensuring they are seeing the results and benefits of working with you. It's about adding a few extra little touches to show you care, like sending a welcome gift, or a little cheeky box of chocolates at Christmas. Because it's all the small touches that get remembered. It's about building your brand reputation by delivering. And delivering well.

So we need to sit down and think of every single touch point a client has with you not just before you secure them but after too. I always find creating a flow chart helpful. And I provide my clients with a step-by-step breakdown of what happens when so that they know what to expect. This way, even if you are busy beavering away they don't feel left in the lurch. They understand the journey of working with you. It's about creating systems and processes that are easy to follow.

Your network is your net worth

It's easy to say what type of brand you are. To stand there and talk the talk. To do everything we've gone through to this point before, but it's your clients who get to experience it all. They're the ones who know if you walk the walk. And if you do, they'll love you for it.

18

LIVING THE BRAND
FOR GOOD

Is this the end? This is probably the point where most people think it's over. That they've done the work and now they can put their feet up and watch the clients roll in. But if you treat your brand that way you will forever be disappointed. This is only the beginning. Remember at the start, in the intro, I spoke about how no logo or website is going to save you. Well, living brand you and these last few chapters prove that. It's not a one stop shop, a quick solution to get something nice and fancy that visually represents you. You have to work on this now every single day. With no excuses, no reasons why something else is more important. Don't forget Mrs Pringle. It's time to continue this work you've done now.

If you think of everything that's been covered in this book, you can't just expect others to know about it. The only way they are going to know, is if you tell them. You have to live this brand now. Yes, it may change. Yes, you may rebrand in a few years. Your business may change direction but essentially the essence stays the same... You are your brand. So when you change, it changes. When you feel like not showing up, it doesn't show up either. Your job now is to spread the word.

When I started writing this book I shared so many stories about myself, the child, the adult, the business woman, the comparer, the overthinker, the unfamiliar woman. And it's all the steps and the processes of my journey that make up the brand that I am today. Your brand has power but only if you allow it. Only if you embrace it. Only if you share your journeys and experiences just as I have, to teach your lessons. Only if you don't slip back into the old ways of trying to be something you think you need to be. A brand is the difference between being a client magnet and scrambling around for people to buy from you. Your brand attracts people, it helps you to become magnetic by showing up as yourself and it will be the only thing that you can guarantee on, in your business.

Because business changes. Marketing tactics change. Strategies change. But you and your brand remain.

Centred, aligned, in sync. Why? Because it's just a representation of who you are, what you want to do. You are now just implementing it, speaking it, sharing it. Without my brand and me being truly comfortable in who I am, I wouldn't be where I am today. Wrapping up a final chapter of a book, selling out programs, helping to change women's lives. Without who I am and what I've learnt from working out all of the steps of this process for myself, I wouldn't be on the same path now. Making waves, bridging the gap between a brand and a business. Helping people realise that they can run successful businesses without having to change who they are. Your brand has power. And if your brand is you then it's time to start believing that YOU HAVE POWER too. Power to create a change. Power to create the life you want to create. Power to be who you are and still make an impact. Power to just be you.

No more glass ceilings

For my first two years of business, I hid under a ceiling. A very large, very big, glass ceiling. No one could see it, no one would have known it was there, except me. I only pushed the true parts of myself a little bit, I only said parts of what I wanted to say. I allowed myself to be an eighth of the woman I wanted to truly show up as every day. I did this out of fear, rejection, worries, influence and more. I did this because even though I'd done this work, I hadn't truly embraced it. I allowed this huge glass ceiling to hang over me. This invisible barrier that, if I hadn't punched my way through it, would have stopped me from doing so many things.

That is the only difference for you now. Because it's a choice to break through. We are not in the corporate world. We get to decide whether we are going to break free and be true to ourselves or not. Whether we say what we truly want to say, share what we truly want to share and be who we truly are. Only you get to decide. We don't live in giant greenhouses. There is space out there for us. No cap. No ceiling. We create this ceiling for ourselves as business women. So we get to decide it's not there anymore.

It's about realising that you have too much to give to be an eighth of yourself. That not everyone will like you, that you might not be everyone's cup of tea, but you won't let the potential impact of that make you live an eighth of a life. It's time now. It's time you take action on all of this. It's time you create the brand you want. The brand you need. It's reachable, touchable, you can see it. Who's with me? Hands on hips, one hand in the air and let's punch through it. Not tip toe in. Punch our way through. Show our superpowers. Show how amazing we are. Show what we've got to offer. Go on. You can do it. You've come this far.

Closing thoughts

I want to leave you with a few thoughts. Ones that I need you to remember when you have days that this all gets a little hard. Which I am not going to lie, it will. This business malarkey is like one big old roller coaster. And there are gonna be dips just as much as there is going to be one big old loop-de-loop. But in those moments, when the dips hit, when it feels like things aren't going to plan, when you start questioning your purpose in this world, I want you to do one thing for me. Pick up the work you've done from this book. Remember your reasons why you do this, what you are trying to achieve, what you bring to the table, who you are as a woman and remember how far you've come. We put so much pressure on ourselves for the next best thing. But what about all we've achieved to date? What about all we have done to help others, no matter how big or small? It's time we give ourselves credit for that. It's time we celebrate that and remember it when we need it the most.

Then, when you've remembered all of what makes you just the most amazing brand, you are going to pick yourself back up, get out there and continue to do the work you were made to do. That you want to do. Because there is no more holding ourselves back. It's time to be seen, be heard and be you. You've got everything you need to soar. Go get it.

ABOUT THE AUTHOR

Nicki James is a personal brand strategist and champion for female entrepreneurs on a mission to release the magic of other women in business- by giving them permission to be themselves. Nicki is helping her clients to show up, get visible and kick imposter syndrome into touch as they step into their true zones of genius and rightful places in the world, so that they can grow successful businesses whilst still celebrating their individuality and true purpose.

Fighting against the misconception that you need to be split personality as a business owner - one person for work, one person for home, Nicki is passionate about empowering female entrepreneurs with confidence and clarity around their marketing helping them see that the rocket fuel that helps them fly - is them. And that the secret sauce they need to grow their business isn't the latest 'marketing magic" - but their individual magic, which needs to be conveyed. She empowers women to unlock their full potential by building a brand that looks, feels and sounds like them.

Sharing stages across the world alongside the likes of Google, being seen in publications such as Stylist, Metro, Grazia and Woman magazine and with an online community and audience of thousands, she is passionate about spreading her message to empower others.

Knowing what it's like to experience rapid growth and the impact truly connecting to your audience has on getting you there, Nicki practices what she preaches and continuously challenges herself to step out of her comfort zone in order to find her full potential. She's found a coaching style that works for her, that she uses with her clients daily as she encourages them to "be a little more you and a lot less them".

Helping her clients powerfully communicate through genuinely showcasing their values, their qualities and their real character, rather than showcasing some over polished, sculpted corporate version of themselves she is turning much of traditional marketing on its head encouraging female entrepreneurs to build a brand based around the woman and not the business as she helps more women cut through the noise in the online space, by claiming their own unique part of it.

With a career that has seen her be involved in the communications of iconic brands such as National Geographic and a creative steer for much loved mag Olive, Nicki is no stranger to the word of creative communication, and she is now known as a champion of female entrepreneurs, promoting visibility.

Nicki has transformed the fortunes of many women, and she is driven by her passion to empower others and help them see that they CAN achieve more than they thought was possible for them - without changing who they are.

Nicki's whole approach to business is driven by her realisation that it is absolutely essential to be YOU to be happy, successful and fulfilled. Nicki's goal is to help as many women as possible to reach their potential. With a range of services from one to one, group programs, masterminds and retreats, Nicki has created a suite of services to ensure she can help women at all different levels.